P9-CEG-984

SLAVES *on* SCREEN

SLAVES
on
SCREEN

Film and Historical Vision

———◆———

NATALIE ZEMON DAVIS

Harvard University Press
Cambridge, Massachusetts
2000

Copyright © 2000 by Natalie Zemon Davis
All rights reserved
Printed in the United States of America
Published by arrangement with Random House Canada,
a division of Random House of Canada Limited, Toronto, Canada
See page 161 for illustration credits

Library of Congress Cataloging-in-Publication Data
Davis, Natalie Zemon, 1928–
Slaves on screen : film and historical vision / Natalie Zemon Davis.
p. cm.
Includes bibliographical references.
ISBN 0-674-00444-2 (alk. paper)
1. Slavery in motion pictures. I. Title
PN1995.9.S557 D38 2000
791.43'655—dc21
00-039687

To the memory of

Julian Leon Zemon
1902–1984
and
Horace Bancroft Davis
1898–1999

CONTENTS

Preface

THE THEMES of *Slaves on Screen* have been entwined in my life for years. When I started my graduate studies a half-century ago, I planned to put my history training to work in documentary film. But then I was caught by voices from the archives and books of the distant past, especially the voices of resistance: of a fifteenth-century lady writer informing her malicious male critics that women had invented "new arts and sciences"; of Protestants marching through the streets of sixteenth-century Lyon singing the Psalms in French, in defiance of the Catholic clergy; of printers' journeymen striking for higher wages and claiming, as "honorable" workers, the right to sit at their masters' tables. I put aside my movie plans and turned instead to the typewriter, the printing press, and the university podium.

In my decades as a historian, I have concentrated on people somehow outside the traditional centers of power or wealth in the early modern period: artisans and their wives, the urban poor, peasant families, women writers and women religious activists, and, most recently, American Indians in New France and Africans living as slaves in the Caribbean and Suriname. In all these cases, I have seen the people not as personifications of heroism or passive victimhood. Rather, they are flesh-and-blood human beings with some agency, shaped by the distinctive circumstances and values of their times, sometimes accommodating, sometimes resisting, sometimes suffering, sometimes escaping, sometimes changing things and trying something new.

By the 1970s, I had new ideas about how to get an understanding of men and women who have usually left us little written evidence about themselves—and these ideas were to take me back to the world of film. I began to see how I could use not only folk tales, folk medicine, and proverbs in my quest, but also carnivals, charivaris (or shivarees, as we call them in North America), and other festivals as well as popular liturgical forms. This approach meant thinking of the cultures of the early modern period in terms of *performance*, of trying to visualize the dramatic unfolding of conflicts and solidarities in a village or city neighborhood. I yearned for a juicy example, where I could be like an anthropologist observing daily experience, rather than putting an account together from a tax record here, a marriage contract there.

At this juncture I came across a description of a 1560 trial written by the judge: a case of imposture in a Pyrenean village, where a man had taken the identity of Martin Guerre for three years or more, deceiving even his wife—or so it was said. "This has got to be a film!" I thought.

In 1980–82 I found myself serving as historical consultant to director Daniel Vigne and scenarist Jean-Claude Carrière for *Le retour de Martin Guerre*. Among the many fruits of working with these talented filmmakers was the chance to see history in extensive play outside the classroom, the scholarly meeting, the professional journal, and the book review. Though the director had the final say, decisions about how the past would look and sound were made in every corner, even by local villagers who decided which of their farm animals to provide. The actors found their own paths to reenacting sixteenth-century lives: some by reading the judge's account or relevant books, others by talking about sensibilities and motives or posture and hand gestures in the days of Martin Guerre. Some entered their roles from the outside, by putting on sixteenth-century dress; others from the inside, starting from "the guts"—or so it seemed with Gérard Depardieu. Watching Depardieu playing the impostor Arnaud du Thil playing Martin Guerre gave me new questions to ask about the definition of self in sixteenth-century France. It was then that I first began to think of historical film as a "thought experiment." Along with the sixteenth-century records of Martin Guerre's village of Artigat, I had the village where we filmed—a surrogate Artigat where we could try out the past.

For me, the story of Martin Guerre finally had to be a book as well as a film. I realized early along that, as good as the film was, it was making a few important departures from the historical record. Furthermore, there were complexities in the evidence that the film, rich and nuanced though it was, could not accommodate. Writing *The Return of Martin Guerre* while consulting on *Le retour de Martin Guerre* introduced me to the differences between telling history in prose and telling history on film. That double experience also convinced me that with patience, imagination, and experimentation, historical narration through film could become both more dramatic and more faithful to the sources from the past.

This conviction was, if anything, strengthened by my seminar at Princeton University in the 1980s and 1990s, History and Film, where the students tried to design films that would be both good cinema and good history. The belief in that possibility informs this book. I take as my example films on slavery and resistance to slavery, a subject at the heart of my current research. The films in *Slaves on Screen* are giving me new eyes with which to look once again at the plantations, uprisings, and manumissions of Suriname.

I

—

Film as Historical Narrative

An encampment just outside the walls of Rome, 71 BCE. A great Roman general confronts the captured gladiator Spartacus, leader of a slave uprising that had defied Rome's legions for two years. "Spartacus. You are he, aren't you?" Spartacus does not speak. "I am Marcus Licinius Crassus," says the general. "You must answer when I speak to you." Spartacus says not a word. The general slaps him. Spartacus spits in the general's face.

An island in the Antilles, in the 1850s. An angry Englishman looks into the face of an ex-slave, once his collaborator in revolt, now his opponent, the captured leader of the rebellious blacks. "Listen to me. It wasn't I who invented this war," the English-man snarls, wanting some response. The black leader stares back in proud silence and spits at the white man.

A sugar plantation in Cuba, 1795. The count sits his most stub-born slave next to him at his dinner table in imitation of Christ and his Apostles. The two men look at each other, resembling in profile Giotto's celebrated painting of Jesus gazing into the face of Judas. "Who am I?" demands the count, "Who am I?" The slave stares in silence, then spits at his master.

The count and his slave Sebastián from *The Last Supper*

THREE REENACTMENTS IN FILM of imagined moments in the long history of slavery and resistance to it: What do we make of them? Do we shrug them off, as Laurence Olivier merely playing the the Roman general, Kirk Douglas Spartacus, and Marlon Brando, the Englishman? Do we note the similarity in all the scenes—the masters seeking acknowledgment, the rebels silent, the spitting—and wonder whether the latter two movies are quoting the first, as filmmakers are wont to do? Or can we go on to ask whether these scenes are also serious efforts to represent conflicts and sensibilities in the history of slavery? Can we cast filmmakers, actors, and viewers as participants in a collective "thought experiment" about the past?

At first glance, this objective may seem to be a difficult one. Readers may well wonder whether we can arrive at a historical account faithful to the evidence if we leave the boundaries of professional prose for the sight, sound, and dramatic action of film. In fact, this question was posed in ancient Greece, well before Spartacus's day, in regard to historical prose and epic poetry. Herodotus and Thucydides had made the switch from poetry to prose in writing down their histories in the fifth century BCE, and it was something of a revolution. Homer had sung with divine inspiration of the quarrels that led to the Trojan War. Herodotus's account of the wars between the Persians and the Greeks was drawn not from a goddess, but from what he had "learned by inquiry (*histories*)." Thucydides, too, wrote of the Peloponnesian War from his own "inquiries," critically comparing accounts and evidence. Poets like Homer were permitted to exaggerate or invent, he explained, to please and engage their listeners, but he wrote only what he had witnessed or discovered from reliable sources.[1]

Decades later Aristotle drew the distinction between poetry and history in another way, stressing less the importance of verse as opposed to prose and more their content and aim. "The historian relates what happened, the poet what might happen . . . Poetry deals with general truths, history with specific events." Thinking of both epic and the tragic theater, Aristotle said that the poet must choose from events, actual or fictitious, and shape them to make a unified story, while the historian must tell whatever has happened within a time period, whether or not things fit neatly together.[2]

These classical distinctions were often blurred in practice. In regard to the many speeches quoted in his history, the rigorous Thucydides explained that he could not remember word for word what he had heard or what had been recounted to him, "so my habit has been to make the speakers say what was in my opinion demanded of them by the various occasions, of course adhering as closely as possible to the general sense of what they really said." This convention of inserting made-up, but appropriate, speeches was followed by European historians into the sixteenth century.

Further, in choosing between conflicting accounts of events, Thucydides might well have been obliged to fall back on what was "possible" in human behavior—in other words, the task that Aristotle assigned to poetry. Historians today still perform this exercise. As for historians simply providing a shapeless account of everything that happens in a period, Aristotle's picture of historical writing was not accurate. Historians picked and chose what to write about then and have done so ever since. History books may not have the same kind of beginning, middle, and end as a Greek tragedy, but they had and have an ordered structure nonetheless.[3]

The ancient contrast between poetry and history, and the crossover between them, anticipate the contrasts and crossovers between historical film and historical prose. Poetry has not only been given the freedom to fictionalize but it brings a distinctive set of *techniques* to its telling: verse forms, rhythms, elevated diction, startling leaps in language or metaphor. The conventions and tools of poetry can limit its use to convey some kinds of historical information, but they can also enhance its power for expressing certain features of the past. For example, Walter Rodney has told the story of slavery and working people in the Caribbean in scholarly social histories. Derek Walcott's *Omeros* gives poetic voice to the sorrow and greatness in these same experiences. His griot laments the seizure of African slaves: "We were the colour of shadows when we came down / with tinkling leg-irons to join the chains of the sea."[4]

———◆———

What is film's potential for telling about the past in a meaningful and accurate way? We can assess it under the same headings used for poetry and history: the subject matter or plot; the techniques for narration and representation; and the truth status of the finished product. Here I will examine "feature films," both those with a central plot based on documentable historical events of resistance to slavery and those with an imagined plot, but where historical events are intrinsic to their action. I choose feature films because they are a more difficult case than documentary films. Feature films are often described as creatures of invention, without significant connection to the experienced world or the historical past. The term "fiction films" is often applied to them in cinema studies, highlighting a contrast between unconstrained imagination in feature films and "truth" in nonfictional documentary. It is precisely this dichotomy that I want to question, not merely because there is a play of invention—of "fictive" crafting—in documentary film, docudrama, and cinéma-vérité (as there is also in prose historical texts), but also because feature films can make cogent observations on historical events, relations, and processes.[5]

In reflecting on film as a medium for presenting history, we should remember, too, that filmmakers have only a hundred years of experience behind them, years marked by rapid technological change in tools and equipment. Historical writers have had more than 2500 years in which to develop different genres, such as political history and historical biography; to widen or narrow their frames, from the history of a village, to the history of an empire, to global history; and to experiment with styles of exposition and proof. Filmmakers have had a century of experience with private, governmental, and institutional sources of funding and with different regimes of censorship. Historians have written over the millennia for many kinds of patrons, sponsors, and political figures, some of whom insisted on sycophantic loyalty, while others encouraged independence. Film is only beginning to find its way as a medium for history.

As for the subject matter of feature films, it is usually said that it must take the form of a concrete, limited story. Edward P. Thompson's *Making of the English Working Class* or Emmanuel Le Roy Ladurie's *Peasants of the Languedoc* or Eugene Genovese's *Roll, Jordan, Roll* could never be transposed to film, so the argument goes, even though each has a collective "hero" and a narrative with a beginning, middle, and end.[6] Instead, a filmmaker inspired by such important books would choose among their myriad examples a craftsman's, peasant, or slave family, and single out a Luddite machine-smashing, a peasant uprising, or a slave escape.

Most historical films are organized around a particular story, even when a grand theme has captured the filmmaker's imagination. *Glory, All Quiet on the Western Front*, and *Saving Private Ryan* all follow a small group of individuals through, respectively, the American Civil War, World War I, and World War II. But we should not rule out other possibilities for cinematic plots. In his *October* of 1928, Sergei Eisenstein pictured the Bolshevik Revolution through mass scenes, symbolic figures or events, and the startling juxtaposition of images. Eisenstein told his film students that they could call an individual a "character," but they could also conceptualize a battleship as a character, or a crowd about to join an uprising, or an enormous unit of the Tsarist army.[7]

In its usual story form, the feature film can recount the past in the mode of historical biography and "microhistory." In microhistory, historians explore a telling example in depth—it might be a striking court case or crime, a dramatic rift or long-term quarrel in a village, a strange rumor and associated panic—and use it to uncover social processes that may be typical of their day or unusual. In their microhistories, films can reveal social structures and social codes in a given time and place, sources and forms of alliance and conflict, and the tension between the traditional and the new. Films can dig deep into family life in the past, one of the most important fields of social history in the late twentieth century. Films can show people at work, from medieval peasants sowing and harvesting, to Chinese dyers staining crimson cloth in their great vats, to early twentieth-century seamstresses bent over their sewing machines. In cinematic biography, films can suggest how and why political decisions are made in different historical regimes, and their consequences. Films can show—or, more correctly, *speculate* on—how the past was experienced and acted out, how large forces and major events were lived through locally and in detail.

Beyond a well-researched plot, the historical power of a film stems from its multiple techniques and resources for narration. Early film theorists might have objected to that word *narration*, for films were said to imitate realities by showing, not telling. In fact, as David Bordwell has pointed out, films both show and tell, and narration covers all the methods used to get a story across.[8] Director Gillo Pontecorvo described his "great moment" in filmmaking as the point "when you have nearly finished the cutting, and you begin to put the music and visual together. In this moment, you see the object and the purpose come alive."[9] This coming together has implications not only for the coherence and beauty of a film but also for the account it gives of the past. The thousands of choices made can all make a difference to the historical narrative: the actors and their interpretation, the locations and sound; the film (black and white, color) and lighting; the ordering of time (flashbacks, jumps, slow motion, cutting from one event to another or presenting them simultaneously) and the ordering of space (close-up, bird's-eye shot, wide angle, movement around a room, view of the same scene from different angles); and the framing devices, objects, and props. These choices all have an impact on what is being stressed or questioned in the film, on the different reactions of participants to what is happening, on explanations for why events have taken place, and on claims for the certainty or ambiguity of the historical account.

Reviewers of historical films often overlook techniques in favor of a chronological summary of the plot or story line and the overall look of the moving picture in terms of costumes and props. These aspects of the film are necessary, to be sure. But viewers respond as well to the film's modes of narration, just as readers respond to the organization and rhetorical disposition of a history book.

As an example of how film technique shapes the historical message let us consider Gillo Pontecorvo's *Battle of Algiers*, made in 1966, not long before he began *Burn!*, a film about slavery and revolt. Pontecorvo portrays the growth of the movement for independence in the casbah of Algiers in the 1950s and the reactions of the French authorities in the European quarter. Though sympathetic to the Algerian cause, the film is remarkably evenhanded, showing the bloody cost of violence on both sides. Viewers see the explosion of National Liberation Front bombs in a café where a baby is eating ice-cream and in a milk bar where young people are dancing, as well as the bombing of Arab families by the police and the ruthless torture of NLF supporters by the paratroopers. The NLF leaders are devoted to a goal they believe is just, and the film tries to win the spectators' assent to that justice. But the viewers also learn that the commander of the French paratroopers was himself a former hero of the anti-Nazi Resistance in France, and that, willing though the commander is to do everything necessary to keep Algeria French, he still respects the courage of his opponents. One NLF leader says presciently to his Algerian comrade, "It's later, when we've won, that the real battle will begin."

The Battle of Algiers, then, is not an epic celebration of national heroism. It achieves its power by smaller gestures, moving or frightening, but close to life: tears on an Arab woman's cheek and sometimes on a man's; the long and troubled glance of a woman, who has just placed a bomb, at the faces of those who will be her victims a few moments later; the sounds of women ululating; the sight of the casbah stairs and the inner courts—where pursuits, attacks, and arrests occur—shown sometimes from way below, sometimes from way above.

The black-and-white film of *The Battle of Algiers* suggested to viewers that they were seeing events as they happened, rather than as they were staged about ten years later. Pontecorvo wanted it to seem this way. As he said:

> There is a necessity for a realistic approach to action, a necessity to represent it as a form of document. It must be accented, more or less, depending on the subject. I pushed this tendency to the limit in *The Battle of Algiers* . . . [There], not only the images, but also the dialogue seems to come from reportage. Everything was filmed with a telephoto lens which gave it a graininess, the look of real events captured spontaneously.[10]

Pontecorvo's success here poses the question of the truth status of historical films. This issue was raised in 1967, when *The Battle of Algiers* was nominated for and won an Academy Award. Pontecorvo made an announcement, which thereafter opened the version of the film with English subtitles: "This dramatic re-enactment of the battle of Algiers contains not one foot of newsreel or documentary film."

———◆———

For historians, these added words are a welcome clarification, fulfilling one of the requirements—honesty—they set for telling about the past. These requirements have developed over the centuries since Herodotus and Thucydides. They were given an increasingly formal structure as historical studies were professionalized in the nineteenth century. In the late twentieth century, influenced in part by certain philosophical and literary currents, they became more nuanced and flexible.

The criteria for writing about history can be summarized quite simply and provide a useful prelude to the exploration of films on slave resistance.[11] First, historians should seek evidence about the past widely and deeply, and should keep their minds as open as they can when they collect and assess it. The expression "open minds" refers to all the attitudes, values, and understandings they bring to a project. An earlier period might have called them "prejudices" or "preconceived notions and judgments"; more recently they have been called "constructions," stemming from things as basic as our language.

These understandings and notions are not to be looked at only as handicaps; they are also our resources and tools for exploration. The danger is that they will blind historians to the different, the strange, the unexpected, and the surprising in their evidence, so they will remake the past in familiar terms, resembling too much the present, or what they have come to expect history to look like. "Keeping one's mind open" means being aware of this temptation and developing techniques for detachment and imaginative perception as historians collect and think. Let the past be the past.

Second, historians should tell readers where they found their evidence and, when it is ambiguous or uncertain or contradictory, they should admit it. Historians have developed various techniques for doing so since the sixteenth century: discussions in the text, commentary in the margins, notes at the bottom of the page or in the back of the book, bibliographies, appendices.[12] Some historians turn to these sections first when they pick up their colleagues' books.

Third, when historians decide what their evidence means and what account they want to give—whether they're explaining causes and consequences, ascribing motives and hopes, describing customs, systems, encounters, and styles, or whatever—they should make clear what they are doing and where they are coming from. They should suggest what assumptions they have made to link kinds of behavior at a certain time or place. If they are interpreting beyond what their evidence strictly offers, they should say so. Phrases such as "we may speculate that . . ." or "one could imagine that . . ." are one way that historians qualify their texts; "Caesar may have thought that . . ." "Cleopatra may have wondered whether . . ." are another. If historians find themselves creating a composite character—for instance, as Eileen Power did in *Medieval People*, using multiple sources to imagine a day in the life of a Carolingian peasant, Bodo, and his wife, Ermentrude[13]— fine, but they should say what they are doing. If they use a counter-factual argument or an imagined event to make a point, fine, but again admit it and explain why it helps. In all these ways, historians can move openly into the realm of the possible, assigned by Aristotle only to the poet.

Fourth, whatever subjective or normative judgments historians make in the course of their historical tale, they should not let them impede their efforts to understand the mental world of all their participants. "Understand, don't judge," declared Marc Bloch and Lucien Febvre, founders of the great Annales school of historical study back in the 1930s. Today, normative elements seem inevitable and not always regrettable in historical writing. Quite apart from mere partisanship, judgments are involved in the choice of subject, approach, and rhetoric. Should it be told as a tragic tale? an ironic tale? Historians can recognize these moral stances and perceptual habits in themselves and acknowledge them, say, in a preface. Whatever their preference, historians are urged to describe a situation from the point of view of the different actors. The old rule might be recast, "Judge if you will, but not without understanding first."

Fifth, historians should not knowingly falsify events even in small matters, or suppress evidence so as to give a wrong impression. Even though imagination, speculation, and "fictive" crafting have their legitimate role in historical research and exposition, they should be identified as such where appropriate. Historians can make mistakes, too. But intentional falsification and tendentious concealment break the historian's promise to readers, present and future, to try to speak true about the past.

———◆———

Historians debate among themselves how narrowly these rules should be interpreted, and they continue to find new ways to live up to them. But tight or loose, are these rules relevant to the historical quality and truth status of feature films?

Let us note two important differences between historical filmmaking and historical book writing. In films, the processes of research, interpretation, and communication are widely dispersed, even if directors put their stamp on the product along the way and in the final editing. Research or research inquiries of a kind are made by scenarists, designers, costume and prop specialists, location seekers, casting directors, actors, composers and arrangers of music, and directors.[14] What the film looks and sounds like will depend on small decisions from many sources—including the interpretive performance of the actors (tightly controlled by some directors, given free rein by others), the style of the directors of photography and music, unexpected events during filming, and post-editing interventions by producers. Such collective creation contrasts with historical book writing, whose cast of characters would extend at most to a few co-authors, student research assistants, an editor and copy editor, and a book designer.

Further, historical film and historians' prose venture into different turfs in regard to claims of truth. Marina Warner, insightful historian of Jeanne d'Arc's life and reputation over the centuries, has extracted multiple and competing images of the young woman as they emerge from her trial and other contemporary documents. In May 1431, after three to four months of trial, Jeanne abjured her heresies: she said she had lied when she claimed to have undertaken her actions at the urgings of God and to have heard the voices of angels and saints, and she admitted she was a sinful and dissolute woman to have worn men's clothing. Three days later she withdrew her recantation and demanded to have her male clothing back.

Warner comments: "In prison after her recantation, Joan realised she had signed away her specialness, and she wanted it back. And the outward sign of her uniqueness was her dress, both for [her judge] Cauchon and for herself." This observation is Warner's interpretation, but one she supports in regard both to the Maid and to the judge by recurrent quotations from the trial record and ample reference to contemporary thought about transvestism. Warner is affirming as true that this trial took place, that certain questions and answers were recorded by the scribes in a document that can be found at the Bibliothèque Nationale de France, and that Jeanne's recorded words support her argument.[15]

In his celebrated *Passion of Jeanne d'Arc* of 1927, the Danish director Carl Theodor Dreyer pictures the trial through a set of extraordinary close-ups, where the ecclesiastical judges (one of them played by Antonin Artaud) circle around Jeanne and her eyes circle around them. Here the claim can only be to what Robert Rosenstone has called "proximate, appropriate characters, situations, and images."[16] But it can still be a well-documented approximation (Dreyer's historical consultant was Pierre Champion, editor of the original trial transcript) and can still help viewers grasp the yawning gap between fifteenth-century doctors of theology and law and an unlettered village woman with strong religious and political affirmations. "What counted [for me]," said

Dreyer, "was getting the spectator absorbed in the past; my means were new . . . All those pictures express the character of [Jeanne] and the spirit of that time."[17]

These are the reasons I am suggesting that historical films can be a thought experiment about the past, involving many participants, sometimes even drawing in the persons living around the location where the film is being shot. And some directors, like Dreyer, care about being faithful to historical evidence. It is true that in 1936 producer Darryl Zanuck crowed jubilantly in a familiar Hollywood mode:

> In *Rothschild* I made Rothschild an English Baron and there never was a Rothschild a Baron. I had the King of England give him the honor, and at this time there was no King of England as the king was in the insane asylum . . . The picture in England got the same wonderful reviews it received in America and no one ever mentioned these technical discrepancies.

But others would agree with Francesco Rosi, director of films about the Sicilian bandit Salvatore Giuliano and the American gangster Lucky Luciano:

> If you choose to narrate something about a real person . . . you cannot invent, in my opinion, but you can interpret. There is a big difference. Why fabricate something just because it makes for more spectacular cinema and an easy way to grab the audience? No, I have all the room I need in my films to interpret the reality and this is the important thing for me, the interpretation of facts.[18]

Historical films extend the experiment in thought, sight, and sound to very large audiences, who react to what they have seen.

John Sayles, director of the excellent historical film *Matewan*, commented a few years ago:

> There's a certain power that comes from history. I mean, I've heard producers say many, many times that the only way a movie is going to work is if the ad says "Based on a true story." Audiences appreciate the fact something really happened. Whether it did or didn't, they're thinking that it did or knowing that it did.[19]

Sayles might better have concluded, "Audiences appreciate the fact something really happened, and they'll wonder after they see the film whether it got the story right." The passive spectator, naively accepting what comes off the movie screen, has disappeared from film theory,[20] and should also disappear from historical criticism of films. Spectators may delight in a historical film, be interested in it or repelled by it; they may replay parts of it in their minds and visualize Raymond Massey when they hear the name Abraham Lincoln, or Anthony Hopkins when they hear that of John Quincy Adams. But they do not believe automatically what they see in a historical film: rather, they ask about it, argue about it, and write letters of protest about it.

As long as we bear in mind the differences between film and professional prose, we can take film seriously as a source of valuable and even innovative historical vision. We can then ask questions of historical films that are parallel to those we ask of historical books. Rather than being poachers on the historian's preserve, filmmakers can be artists for whom history matters.

2

Resistance and Survival: Spartacus

S LAVERY has been a subject of films since the early days
of cinema. In 1913 the Italian Ernesto Pasquali celebrated
the Roman gladiator Spartacus, and two years later D.W.
Griffiths electrified American movie-goers and international
directors with the *Birth of a Nation*, his film on Civil War and
Reconstruction. From the beginning, films expressed a range of
attitudes toward slaves similar to that found in the historical writing of the day. In Pasquali's film, Spartacus was a heroic figure
as he inspired his fellow slaves to revolt; likewise W.E.B. Du
Bois, in a pioneering 1896 book on the African slave trade,
found heroic qualities in the leaders of slave revolts in the American South in the eighteenth century. In Griffiths's film, black
people were laughing and happy when slaves, trusting and sup-
portive of their masters; once freed, they were violent, decep-
tive, and sexually predatory. They appeared this way in history
books written by Woodrow Wilson, who had been Griffiths's
major source for the film and later arranged a showing at the
White House.[1]

After World War II, another parallel emerged between film and historical scholarship: a fresh interest in resistance to slavery by slaves themselves. In 1953 a new *Spartacus* was made in Italy, followed by two more Italian films on the same subject in the next decade.[2] In 1954 Kenji Mizoguchi, one of Japan's greatest directors, brought out *Sancho the Bailiff,* a beautiful film drawn from a medieval legend about a well-born brother and sister who are sold into slavery; through courage and sacrifice, they bring freedom to their fellows. "It has been retold by the people for centuries," Mizoguchi says in his opening, "and is treasured today as one of the epic folk tales of our history." As the next decade opened, Stanley Kubrick's *Spartacus* began playing to huge audiences, bringing a comfortable margin of profit to Hollywood's Universal Studios. A few years later it was the turn of Gillo Pontecorvo's *Burn!* (*Queimada*), a narrative of anticolonial and antislavery revolts on the mythical Caribbean island Queimada. And there were still more slave films to come in the next decades.

In historical writing, studies of slave resistance, both ancient and modern, had been published before World War II, though they were usually limited to specialist readers. Then books with wider resonance began to appear about Brazil, the Caribbean, and North America. *Black Jacobins,* published in 1938 by the Trinidadian polymath C.L.R. James, connected the 1791 revolution on Saint-Domingue/Haiti to events in France and the new United States. During the war, Herbert Aptheker published his Columbia University doctoral thesis, *American Negro Slave Revolts,* which considered various forms of resistance, from theft to rebellion. He argued that slave revolts and fear of their recurrence had consequences for policy, political thought, the abolition movement, and class alliance among the poor. In particular, he stressed the attitude of the slaves themselves:

This study has attempted to meet the need . . . of depicting in realistic terms the response of the American Negro to his bondage. The data herein presented make necessary the revision of the generally accepted notion that his response was one of passivity and docility . . . On the contrary . . . discontent and rebelliousness were not only exceedingly common, but, indeed, characteristic of American Negro slaves.[3]

Aptheker's American Negroes bore little resemblance to the people serving the white folks in *Gone with the Wind*, a film that opened while he did his research.

After the war, studies on slavery multiplied, and, increasingly, they were comparative and interdisciplinary. In 1960, the same year as Kubrick's *Spartacus*, M. I. Finley brought out a collection of essays, *Slavery in Classical Antiquity*, where he and other scholars revealed the vast extent of slave labor outside the small family farm or workshop: Greece and Rome could be called "slave societies." In 1966 David Brion Davis's *Problem of Slavery in Western Culture* appeared, a remarkable examination, over many centuries and countries, in which he asked why antislavery—the belief that slavery was an unacceptable human relation—took so long to emerge as a widely held view. In 1969, the same year as Pontecorvo's *Burn!*, Laura Foner and Eugene Genovese published a volume of essays, *Slavery in the New World*, about the significance of slavery and racism in different economies of the Americas. A few years later, readers were absorbed in Genovese's splendid study of the slaves themselves, *Roll, Jordan, Roll: The World the Slaves Made*. Here he portrayed the ways of life of African Americans on Southern plantations, including their reactions to masters: accommodation, self-assertion, running away, and revolt.[4]

This parallel in subject matter between film producers and historians was in part coincidental. A slave uprising could be just what was needed for a film industry that continued to flourish worldwide on epic and warfare. Similarly, slave revolts and other forms of slave resistance satisfied social historians who were turning their attention to the actions and initiative of the lower orders and the poor—whether slave, free, peasant, farmer, artisan, or factory worker. Working people were not mere victims of oppression, but also shapers of their world, and sometimes they resisted its conditions. Political events and moral questions after World War II turned filmmakers and historians alike to thinking about forms of resistance: the legacy of horror and massive death from the war, anticolonial movements throughout the world, Cold War issues, civil rights agitation in the United States, the apartheid regime in South Africa, and persistent or new forms of totalitarian government.

Irrespective of their present-day origins, what do films about slavery tell us of the past?[5] The five films examined in this book (and listed only by their directors here) span almost forty years in their making: Kubrick's *Spartacus* and Pontecorvo's *Burn!* from the 1960s, Tomás Gutiérrez Alea's *The Last Supper* from the 1970s, and Steven Spielberg's *Amistad* and Jonathan Demme's *Beloved* from the 1990s. Directly or indirectly, they have a bearing on several of the questions about slave resistance that historians have been asking over the decades.

At the time *Spartacus* was made, historians were debating whether a characteristic personality had been shaped by the conditions of slavery in different settings. Were slaves all docile? rebellious? or a bit of both?[6] Soon attention shifted to a more significant matter—the character of slave revolts. Were they frequent and did they take place in distinctive localities? Who joined and led them? What set them off and what traditions or beliefs legitimated them? Revolts are not an everyday affair, after all, and leaders have to be convincing. What did revolts accomplish? Did they change anything for better or for worse in social relations and attitudes, or did life return to its usual train?

Finally, historical inquiry widened its view of slave resistance beyond uprisings to less violent forms of protest. Slaves might develop magic, religions, naming patterns, and songs of their own. They might defend their own family life, or steal time and goods from the master and mistress, before they ever decided to run away.

As exemplary stories, the five films considered here address some of these questions and not others, and the answers they offer to viewers vary in historical significance. But their pictures of how slavery was lived, resisted, fought, and remembered are sometimes insightful and novel, engaging spectators in fresh dialogue with the past.

§§§

In 1957 the actor and producer Kirk Douglas read Howard Fast's novel *Spartacus* and decided it would make "a terrific film."

> Spartacus was a real man, but if you look him up in history books, you find only a short paragraph about him. Rome was ashamed; this man had almost destroyed them. They wanted to bury him. I was intrigued with the story of Spartacus the slave, dreaming of the death of slavery, driving into the armor of Rome the wedge that would eventually destroy her.

Douglas might have been awed by the extent of Rome's empire, but, pondering its ruins, he saw "thousand of slaves carrying rocks, beaten, starved, crushed, dying. I identify with them. As it says in the Torah: 'Slaves were we unto Egypt.' I come from a race of slaves. That would have been *my* family, *me*."[7]

The historical appeal of Spartacus to Howard Fast had been different. In prison in 1950 for contempt of Congress (he had refused to answer questions before the Un-American Activities

Committee), he meditated on the slave as he "began more deeply than ever before to comprehend the full agony and hopelessness of the underclass." He wondered, too, why Rosa Luxemburg had chosen the name "Spartacists" for her revolutionary party in Berlin in 1918. Once released, he read about ancient Rome in classical encyclopedias and old volumes on slavery so that his story "could at least approximate the truth." It was a rapid education: he left Mill Point Federal Prison in September 1950 and completed the manuscript by June 1951.[8] When no commercial publisher would risk taking on a book by Fast, he printed it himself. *Spartacus* was an immediate success.

If Fast wrote well as a novelist, he was a disaster as a scenarist. In early 1958 Kirk Douglas and his Bryna Productions turned to the talented Dalton Trumbo, who was also blacklisted because of his defiance of the Un-American Activities Committee but was writing screenplays under a pseudonym. Trumbo transformed a book organized as fragmentary reminiscences about Spartacus, told after his death, into a chronological narrative of Spartacus's life. If he did any further historical reading as he wrote and rewrote his screenplay, it does not show in the finished product. But he surely had social, psychological, and moral concerns that he wanted to work through in the setting of the late Roman Republic. As Cleo Trumbo said of her husband's writing, he spent his early years "revealing the ultimate pain of the victim" and his last years "exploring the ultimate evil of the oppressor." *Spartacus* seems to stand right at that transition: immediately on its completion, he began his novel *Night of the Aurochs*, a first-person narrative of an unrepentant German Nazi who, among other actions, imprisoned a Jewish woman with whom he had had an affair.[9]

Trumbo's moral universe was not wholly polarized: "He recognized evil in everyone, including himself." Perhaps oppressors could change. He had already written a film script about the

Spanish conquest of Mexico in which Cortés wondered on his deathbed if he had not done wrong. During the making of *Spartacus*, Trumbo discussed moral questions with the actors playing Batiatus, the owner of the gladiator school, and the Roman senator Gracchus, both opponents of Spartacus who exhibit some humanity after the defeat of the slave rebels.[10]

Kirk Douglas assembled an impressive cast to perform along with him as Spartacus, all of them with experience in historical films. Laurence Olivier was to play Crassus, the wealthy patrician who would ultimately command the victorious legions against the slave army. Charles Laughton played Gracchus, a fictional figure in both the novel and the film: as Crassus's political opponent in the Senate, he was rich, corrupt, and an eloquent defender of the Roman plebs. Peter Ustinov was cast as Batiatus, proud of the achievements of his gladiator training school, always alert to money making, ironically obsequious to his social betters. Jean Simmons was brought in to portray Spartacus's loyal companion and lover, Varinia, while Tony Curtis was given the role of a young slave poet, Antoninus, a "singer of songs" and performer of magic tricks. By all accounts, Olivier, Laughton, and Ustinov were arguing about and changing their lines throughout the shooting. As Ustinov described it, "I rewrote all the scenes I had with Laughton, we rehearsed at his home or mine . . . The next day we arranged the studio furniture to conform to what we had engineered."[11]

Spartacus is an excellent example of the multiple small decisions and actions that shape a film. Were any of these decisions inspired by an explicit historical concern—not merely "I don't want to say this line" but rather "I don't believe a Roman slave would say such a line"? Douglas said in reminiscence, "I wanted everything about *Spartacus* to be special and authentic." Perhaps this criterion applied to his thoughts about performance as well as to clothing, coiffures, and props. He had even hoped to suggest the gulf between slaves and masters by having the former have American accents and the latter British accents, but this notion was thwarted when the English Jean Simmons was cast as Varinia.[12]

These stars were directed by a young man named Stanley Kubrick, who turned thirty-one in the course of the filming. Two years earlier he had made an outstanding black-and-white film about World War I, *Paths of Glory*, produced by Kirk Douglas's firm and with Douglas in the leading role. When the director initially hired for *Spartacus* did not work out after a week of shooting, Douglas and Universal Studios summoned Kubrick to take over. For a year in California and, for the battle scenes, in Spain, Kubrick directed the shooting and editing of a multimillion-dollar film whose story had come to him from elsewhere. He regretted doing a film, he said later, "over which [he] did not have complete control" and about whose plot he had reservations.[13] Still, Kubrick's characteristic style and talents are expressed in the visual achievement of the film. They are important sources of its historical value.

To set a film in the past (or in the future) had intrinsic advantages for Kubrick. "The basic purpose of a film," he thought, was "illumination . . . showing the viewer something he can't see any other way." This goal could best be achieved by leaving one's own backyard. A film taking place in another time also "removes the environmental blinkers . . . and gives . . . a deeper and more objective perspective." Several years after making *Spartacus*, Kubrick decided to make a film about Napoleon. It would speak both to the fascination of the past—to the whole career of this man who had "molded the destiny of [his] time"—and to present-day concerns about power, social revolution, and war. But it had to be accurate, "to get the feeling of what it was like to be with Napoleon," "to capture the reality [of battle] on film." To achieve this authenticity, Kubrick said he had gone through hundreds of books in English and French, arranged for consultation with a historian at Oxford, and put twenty people to work making designs from paintings and written descriptions of weapons, dress, and the like. Unfortunately, the film never found a producer.[14]

Some such beliefs and practices must have informed Kubrick's earlier period as director of *Spartacus.* We know he sent off one of his own scriptwriters to Appian's *Roman History* for detail on the final battle between Spartacus's slaves and Crassus's legions. He also urged the composer Alex North to learn what he could about Roman music; failing that—and, given the state of knowledge about Roman music at that date, failure was certain—he should seek inspiration from Prokofiev's score for *Alexander Nevsky.*[15] Kubrick may have had the most genuinely *historical* sensibility of any of the shapers of *Spartacus.*

§§§

What is the film story of Spartacus? *Spartacus* opens with an overture of North's music, an operatic effect, and introduces its subject with an overvoice saying, "In the last century before the birth of the new faith called Christianity . . . the Roman republic stood at the very center of the civilized world . . . Yet even at the zenith of her pride and power, the republic lay fatally stricken with a disease called human slavery." Spartacus, a slave from Thracia, is seen toiling miserably in the mines of Libya, where he is condemned to die for attacking a cruel overseer. Instead, he is purchased by Lentulus Batiatus, who seeks spirited slaves for his gladiator school.

Taken to the school in Capua, Spartacus is trained along with other vigorous slaves from Gaul, Africa, and elsewhere, and given a woman for company, Varinia, a slave from Britannia. Crassus visits the school with his sister and another patrician couple, and the women request two private combats to the death.

Spartacus is paired with the African, Draba. Spartacus has previously told another gladiator, "I'd fight if I have to . . . I'd kill. I'd try to stay alive," and now he fights hard. Draba wins the combat, but instead of finishing off Spartacus, he lunges with his trident at Crassus and his party. Crassus slices his neck, and Batiatus and his arrogant trainer Marcellus have Draba's body hung upside down in the slaves' quarters.

The following day at their noonday meal, the slaves revolt. They kill Marcellus and the guards, and, while Batiatus escapes, break out of the school grounds in joy and release.

For the next part of the film, the camera alternates between two different stories. One is the movement of Spartacus's people down the Italian peninsula, their numbers swollen by thousands of slaves from the great estates and town houses—men, women, and children—who join them as they march. Among them is the young poet Antoninus, Crassus's personal slave, who now becomes part of Spartacus's circle. One early battle pits Spartacus's followers against the Roman civic troops sent to put down the revolt. Underestimating the skill and daring of "mere slaves," the troops are slaughtered in a night ambush.

On the whole, the slaves live with good community spirit, improvising what they need, training men and women for battle, and amassing treasure donated or seized along the way. Spartacus arranges with an agent of the Cilician pirates off the coast of southern Italy to pay for 500 boats to transport all the slaves back to their homes. Meanwhile, Spartacus and Varinia deepen their love, and Varinia tells Spartacus she is pregnant.

The other story is set in Rome in the Senate, where the senators hear the increasingly shocking reports of the slaves' military successes, one of them against Julius Caesar, and their burning of estates. Gracchus and Crassus both want the revolt put down, but they maneuver against each other for power in the Senate and in the baths: the popular faction against the patrician. After Crassus wins out, he is assigned supreme command of all the legions to be used against the slaves. He is also named first consul of Rome.

Meanwhile, the mass of runaway slaves reaches the Mediterranean, only to have Spartacus discover that the Cilicians have been bribed by Crassus and that no boats are available. Turning back toward Rome, they meet the enormous army led by Crassus, with support coming in from the troops of Pompey and Lucullus. Now the slaves are defeated. Crassus seeks Spartacus among the corpses and the prisoners, but fails to find him. Batiatus decides not to help him, and the surviving male slaves all shout "I am Spartacus." Crassus takes Varinia and her new-born son back to his estate as slaves. He orders the crucifixion of all the 6000 male prisoners along the Appian Way to Rome, leaving two suspicious ones—Antoninus and Spartacus, whom he does not recognize—to the very last.

The film then moves to Rome, where Crassus tries in vain to persuade his slave Varinia to love him. In a night scene he sets Antoninus and Spartacus—whose identity he now realizes—against each other in a last combat. Spartacus kills Antoninus rather than let him suffer the agony of crucifixion. At the same time, Gracchus has paid Batiatus to get Varinia and her son from

Crassus's house. Savoring his revenge against Crassus, Gracchus sends them on their way to Gaul with letters of manumission and safeguard. As Batiatus takes Varinia from Rome, she sees Spartacus in his last agony on the cross. She shows him his son and tells him the boy is free, just before Spartacus dies.

§§§

Though slaves are the main interest in this book, how is political life among the senators represented in *Spartacus*? The writings of Cicero, Julius Caesar, Sallust, and later historians record that the senators had much on their minds in the years before and after 73–71 BCE. During the slave revolt itself, a civil war between Roman leaders and armies in Spain was just coming to an end; troops had to be sent to Asia Minor against Mithridates, who was challenging Roman control in the East, and against his allies, the Cretan pirates; and factional struggles in the Senate were intense. The general features of that political culture are suggested in the film: the importance of high birth, riches, and family alliance to a role in the Senate; the existence of cliques or parties (called "friendship" by those who formed them and "faction" by their enemies); the bestowal of bribes (called "gifts" by those who gave them); and the use of personal armies, loyal to the generals who recruited and rewarded them, for political advancement. Conflict in the late republic was organized around a "popular" party and a party of the "best" or the "aristocrats," and the danger of tyranny was often proclaimed in political speeches. We see or hear these factions in a general way in the film.[16]

The trouble with *Spartacus* is that it assigns these properties of political life too rigorously to one side or the other. It personifies them misleadingly through leaders who were not even present. The great days of the Gracchi brothers as tribunes of the people, with their actions for agrarian reform, had ended with the death of the younger Gracchus back in 121. There was no Gracchus consul in Spartacus's time. Howard Fast, and later Dalton Trumbo, simply chose a name that viewers might recognize in the hope that it would give the "popular" party the luster of the earlier period. Also wholly invented for the film was the military role of Julius Caesar; at least Caesar was alive during the events, for he had the office of tribune of the soldiers in 71 BCE. In the film, only Gracchus is accused publicly of corruption; in fact, gifts and bribes were passed by all the factions, as everyone knew. The aristocratic Crassus is accused of seeking dictatorship; in fact, intrigue to take control of the state was embarked on by both parties, and each reproached the other, with good reason, for seeking tyranny.[17] What can be said for the film is that the contrived characters are well acted: Laughton's "warm, fleshy integrity" built the person of the sensuous, popular Gracchus; Olivier's "knifelike . . . linear performance" created a "glacial patrician," a Crassus full of ambition.[18]

Although scholars know a lot about slavery in Rome, they have little information about the revolt led by Spartacus from 73 to 71 BCE. The slave population of Italy had increased in the second century BCE, fed mostly by prisoners of war or piracy, and to some extent by condemned criminals and the children of slave women.[19] Roman slavery was primarily agricultural. In the central part of the peninsula the great farms, or *latifundia*, were worked mostly by slaves, while the female slaves did the household tasks. The southernmost part of the peninsula and Sicily were cattle-raising country, and here the male slaves were herders. As they roamed the land with their animals, they often had to live off free peasants and earned a reputation as bandits. Where there were mines, as in the silver mines of Roman Spain, thousands of men worked in chains in appalling conditions. Town slaves, in contrast, lived in their masters' houses, and might be involved in trade and crafts.

Of this extensive world of labor, the film *Spartacus* depicts two extremes—miners and gladiators—and then only by giving Spartacus an alternative past. He began, according to the historical sources we have, not as a slave's son working in the mines but as a free Thracian fighting as a Roman soldier. After he was taken prisoner, he was sold by his captives to be a gladiator.[20] If this information is true, it provides background for his later military success.

The film also shows us the omnipresent world of domestic slavery, especially the sexual uses of slaves. Batiatus's guards leeringly spy on the gladiators' relations with the women sent to their cells. Batiatus's guest casually lifts Varinia's skirt for a look as she passes, and teases his sister about her fondness for her tall litter-bearers. Gracchus revels affectionately in his access to all his house slaves. Crassus tries to entice both Varinia and his man-servant Antoninus (the latter scene was cut from the American version), and by Roman custom he would have had the right simply to make them do his bidding. In Roman thought about slavery, writes the classicist Keith Bradley, "it is taken without question that slaves can and do become objects of sexual gratification for both the men and women who own them."[21]

Spartacus extends the erotic desire into the realm of violence. The patrician women who select Spartacus and Draba for combat are aroused by the event. The killing of Spartacus and the possession of Varinia become equivalent triumphs for Crassus. Such a representation fits with the interest of both Trumbo and Kubrick in the eroticism of power, and sexual excitement may well have been one of the elements in the Roman attachment to blood sports. Later, during the imperial period, both literature and gossip refer to patrician women who were attracted by gladiators.

But gladiator games between humans had other functions as well.[22] They were initially a funeral rite celebrated publicly by the great families of Rome. As such, they draw from the tradition of agonistic games to pacify the gods at the time of death and to glorify the memory of the deceased—an extreme form of lavish display. By the second century BCE, gladiator training schools had sprung up centered at Capua. In Spartacus's day, prominent families demonstrated their power, as well as their desire to make a gift (*munus*) to the Roman plebs, by sponsoring the games at funerals and other public events. These occasions were an important step in political advancement: only a few years after Spartacus's revolt, Caesar sponsored a magnificent show of 320 pairs, fighting to commemorate his father's death years before.[23]

The gladiators themselves in this period were slaves and criminals of low birth whose offense was not serious enough to warrant immediate execution. (Some free men became gladiators during the late republic, and under the empire a few women entered the arena.) They were, as the film portrays, extensively trained with distinctive weapons and specially clad for combat. The winning gladiators were both looked down upon as dishonorable slaves and admired. They were crowned at victory, and their names and scores were scratched on the walls at Pompeii and elsewhere.[24]

This cluster of attitudes and ambivalences is missing from *Spartacus*, partly because the film shows no formal public games (a cliché, to be sure, in the usual epic film on Rome) but only private ones. Instead, the film invites viewers to imagine the gladiator's predicament, as he is forced to fight and kill a person against whom he has no grievance and whom he might even like. "Gladiators don't make friends," Draba says the first day Spartacus arrives, but the African's example in the arena teaches Spartacus and the other gladiators of the possibility of brotherhood. Later, Spartacus puts a stop to a vindictive combat that his somewhat drunken fellows have organized between two slave owners seized along the march: "I swore that if I ever got out of [the gladiator school], I'd die before I'd watch two men fight to the death again . . . What are we becoming? Romans?"

Evidence from the Roman world supports the film's identification of the gladiator's predicament, but not all its proposed solutions. On the one hand, gladiators did sometimes work themselves up to a killing mood by shouting abuse at each other before the match, and inscriptions bear witness to long-term feuds between them and calls for vengeance. But friendships also sprang up among them, with gladiators choosing to spare a victim at the moment of choice in hopes that they would be spared in the same circumstances. (And, indeed, sponsors of combats sometimes let this happen.) They also paid for each other's tombs and memorial inscriptions.[25] Thus, Draba's initial advice not to have friends and his subsequent change of heart in the film are both plausible.

On the other hand, a revulsion against blood sports was unusual in the Romanized world of Spartacus's day, except among small communities such as the Jews of Rome. Could the historical Spartacus have had such views? The combat of the slave owners, though perhaps possible, is an invented episode in the film and can serve only to pose a question about Spartacus and his fellows. The real Spartacus had no fundamental objection to excessive vindictive bloodshed. When the gladiator Crixus, Spartacus's second in command, was killed in battle, Appian reports that "[Spartacus] sacrificed three hundred Roman prisoners of war in honour of Crixus."[26]

Whatever the precise triggering events, the gladiators at Batiatus's school were determined to get away. Plutarch says that Batiatus was "unjust," that two hundred gladiators planned an escape, and that, although their plot was uncovered, more than seventy managed to get out, armed with kitchen axes and skewers. Then, instead of dispersing in the countryside and trying to live as free men, as most runaway slaves would do, the gladiators stayed together, chose Spartacus as their leader along with two others, seized arms, and set up camp on Mount Vesuvius.[27] How did these men legitimate their actions to themselves? And what made them believe in Spartacus as their leader?

The film answers the first of these questions in universalistic terms. In his final speech to the men and women in his camp, Spartacus simply says:

> I'd rather be here a free man among brothers, facing a long march and a hard fight, than to be the richest citizen of Rome, fat with food he didn't work for and surrounded by slaves . . . As long as we live, we must stay true to ourselves. I do know that we're brothers, and I know that we're free.

He does not use glaringly anachronistic phrases of the eighteenth century—the natural rights language of the Enlightenment—but neither does he counter the justifications of slavery so widely held in the first century BCE—the belief in the natural inferiority of "barbarian" peoples compared with Greeks and Romans. The latter view was opposed by a few ancient voices, who said no one was born a slave by nature.[28] Trumbo may have wanted no phrases that would impede the spectators of his own day from identifying with Spartacus's struggle and from seeing its continuing resonance for America and the world in the late 1950s. Kubrick, never a fan of extensive dialogue when it was not necessary, may have wanted to keep things as simple as possible: a good shot of companionate behavior among the masses of disparate slaves could undermine the claims about "barbarians" just as well. Whatever the case, Spartacus's language ends up thin in its timelessness.

Similarly with Spartacus's charisma, as treated in the film. He is shown as a splendid fighter, brave, straight-spoken, encouraging, and handsome. Spartacus may well have had these qualities—Plutarch says of him, "he not only possessed great courage and bodily strength, but was more intelligent and nobler than his fate as a slave would allow"[29]—but they are also general and familiar traits, with no surprise or specificity from the late Roman Republic.

The historical record offers interesting possibilities here. Though slave revolts were not a frequent event over the many centuries of Roman slavery, there had been important uprisings in the century before Spartacus.[30] Around 185 BCE and after, a wave of religious movements dedicated to the god Bacchus swept through parts of Italy, permitting slave and free to worship together without constraint. These gatherings were associated with "conspiracies" of slave herdsmen in the south, who took to the roads in acts of "banditry." Then in 137–35 and 104–2, major slave rebellions occurred on the island of Sicily. In both cases the leaders were wonder-workers who received messages from the gods and foretold the future. In the first revolt, the Syrian slave Eunus was told by a Syrian goddess that he would be king and that she sanctioned the revolt; he and his rebel slaves set up a kingdom of "Syrians" on Sicily. Of the two leaders of the second slave uprising, Salvius was a diviner who had played ecstatic flute music at women's religious festivals, while the Cilician Athenion, an estate manager for his owners, foretold the future from the stars. Both were chosen "kings" by assemblies of slaves in their region.

Some memory of these events was surely passed on among slave populations in Italy, including those in Capua, where there had been a brief uprising during the Second Slave War. Traditions of past revolts could provide legitimation for further slave uprisings in Spartacus's time and also remind people of the signs for recognizing a great leader. Sure enough, in one of the scraps of evidence about Spartacus from Plutarch, we hear a story about the mysterious events that transpired when he was brought to Rome to be sold:

> A snake appeared and wound itself round his face as he was asleep, and his wife, who came from the same tribe as Spartacus and was a prophetess and initiated into the ecstatic cult of

Dionysus, stated that it signified that a great and fearful power would accompany him to a lucky conclusion. This woman was living with him at the time [of the revolt of the gladiators] and ran away with him.[31]

Spartacus had the divine sanction enjoyed by earlier leaders of slave resistance, here provided by his Thracian wife.

Religious sacrifice was also carried on during the slave campaigns by the women. The model for rulership among Spartacus and his followers was not kingly, as in Sicily, but republican: Spartacus took over the horse and the fasces (bundle of rods symbolizing the authority of the Roman Senate) of a defeated Roman commander, and he debated strategy with Crixus and one other leading gladiator. As for Spartacus's goals, at one moment he definitely tried to lead the slaves out of Italy so they could return to their places of birth in Thrace, Gaul, Germany, and elsewhere (though by the northern route over the Alps, not by the Mediterranean, as in the film), but at another he seems to have sought a place to settle within Italy to establish a polity, as the Sicilian rebels had tried to do decades before.[32]

Spartacus the film says nothing of past slave revolts inspiring the gladiators, but gives promise only of the hopes and fears that the name of Spartacus will call forth in the future. As for religion, it is almost ignored among the slaves and is given short shrift among the senators, who in fact used ceremony and divination extensively in political life.[33] "I imagine a god of slaves," Spartacus says once to Varinia, "and I pray . . . for a son who will be born free." Here again the filmmakers seem to have wanted a more "universal" and presumably more accessible Spartacus. But in omitting the snake coiled around his head and the visionary prophetess at his side, they let a more memorable and more powerful Spartacus slip away.

§§§

In weighing *Spartacus* next to the historical record, which has its own uncertainties, I have given a mixed report—some successes, some missed opportunities, some failures. But in four ways *Spartacus* has been outstanding in depicting important social processes and critical experiences of the past. They stem from myriad acts of research, interpretation, and imagination by many people involved in the film, but are finally put together by Kubrick's camera and editing.

The first is the portrayal of the gap between high and low, between free and slave. It is seen in differences in gait, movement, and posture. It is seen in the differences in color: the bordered white togas of the senators in their severe white chamber contrast with the single-hued tunics, brown wool cloaks, and rough furs of the slaves in Spartacus's army as they walk through leafy or snowy landscapes. It is seen in differences in oratory before the last battle, as Kubrick cuts rapidly between Crassus making grand promises to his legions and the citizens of Rome, and Spartacus addressing his people with chastened realism and firm belief in their cause, if not in their victory.

That divisive social space is shown also through the literal movement of Kubrick's camera from high to low, a technique he had used to powerful effect in *Paths of Glory*, where the action shifted from the general's chateau on a hill to the men below in the trenches.[34] In the private combat ordered by Crassus, he and his elegant guests are comfortably ensconced well above the small arena in which Spartacus and Draba fight (see page 26). When Draba suddenly attacks the Romans, the greatest surprise is his jump upward—a difficult leap that connects the two worlds through violence.

A second achievement of *Spartacus* is the depiction of the gladiator school. The harsh trainer, Marcellus—himself once a gladiator and now free—summons the men with a whistle and puts them through their terrible paces in a brilliantly choreographed movement, against a background of harsh and choppy brass and percussion music. To show the men where to aim, to kill fast or slowly, or to maim, the trainer paints different colors on Spartacus's chest and body. Meanwhile, Spartacus cranes his neck to try to get a look at Varinia. This whole sequence, including the conversations about friendship and killing, summons the modern spectator to imagine the pain and tension of the gladiator slave.

Kubrick dwelt on the terrors and fascination of violence in several of his films, from sadism to large battles. A third achievement of *Spartacus* is the representation of the final battle. Spartacus and his thousands of men and women stand with their weapons on a hill and watch Crassus's legions fall into place over another hill across the valley. We look at the legions both close up, as Crassus watches his men, and especially from a distance, through the eyes of Spartacus and his waiting fighters. By an astonishing wide-angle shot, the legions are seen filing over the hill and forming bands, moving forward like a giant symmetrical insect, one, then another, then another and more. The camera takes its time. Here, before Spartacus's eyes, is Rome's power in an unending supply of ordered men, returning and returning no matter how many battles the slaves have won.

The battle itself begins dramatically as the legions move like a rolling, foaming wave and the slave army surprises them with fire weapons—recreated by Kubrick from Appian's description. Then it becomes a chaos of fighting and close combat, which Kubrick cuts quickly to move to a silent denouement with the dead bodies of slaves spread over a vast field. Several years later, in talking of his plans for *Napoleon*, Kubrick said that he wanted to "communicate the essence of the battles to the viewer," to show their "organizational beauty . . . their sordid reality . . . and their human consequences."[35] He accomplished some of these ambitions earlier in *Spartacus*.

The final historical achievement of the film may seem unlikely, for it grows out of the Hollywood-style romantic relation between Spartacus and Varinia and the arrival of their son. Spartacus's actual wife was said to be a Thracian prophetess, as we have seen. She was probably quite different from the steadfast and tender Varinia of the film, whose idyllic interludes with Spartacus take place several times during the revolt. Their conversations have the same "timeless" ring already noted in Spartacus's speeches. Whether Spartacus actually had a son, no one knows. He was reported to have died in battle, however, not to have been among the 6000 men crucified along the Appian Way, as he is in the film.

Where lies the historical value in scenes that seem concocted only to satisfy a twentieth-century sensibility? Spartacus's son, shown to him by Varinia just before he dies on the cross, is usually interpreted as a symbol of hope for the future and for resistance in the wake of the failed uprising. Yet, somewhat by accident, the filmmakers hit on something deeply important to the slaves themselves in their own lifetime.

By Roman law, slaves had no right to marry, and a slave woman's children belonged to her master, not to her. In fact, slaves did set up unions of their own called *contubernia* and cared for their children, who they hoped would take care of them when they were old and commemorate them when they died. The masters often had other plans, however; for if they tolerated and sometimes encouraged slaves' "marriages" for the sake of the labor it would bring, they also separated husband from wife and mother from child by sale. These family ties, when they could be maintained, meant much to the slaves, as can be seen in commemorative inscriptions and in the efforts of freed persons to arrange for the manumission of enslaved relatives.[36]

In the film, then, the presence of children snuggling close to their parents at Spartacus's camp is not a mere sentimental touch but the representation of a form of slave resistance. Both Spartacus and Varinia are said in the film to have been sold when they were thirteen. The survival of Spartacus's son in his mother's arms

and the announcement that he is free—the last sight that Spartacus sees and the last words he hears in the film—are victories that would have been recognized by slaves in his own day.

Interestingly enough, Kubrick's two children were born during the making of *Spartacus*. Kubrick, who rarely expressed his feelings and had little use for happy endings, said after the birth of his second daughter in 1960: "When you get right down to it, the family is the most primitive and visceral and vital unit in our society. You may stand outside your wife's hospital room during childbirth uttering, 'My God, what a responsibility! . . . What am I doing here?' and then you go in and look down at the face of your child and—zap!—that ancient programming takes over and your response is one of wonder and joy and pride."[37]

3

Ceremony and Revolt:
Burn! _and_ The Last Supper

FROM ANCIENT ROME we move to the Caribbean in the late eighteenth and early nineteenth centuries. Here the countries of Western Europe had established their colonies from the sixteenth century on, crowding out most of the Amerindian peoples and their economies in favor of sugar, coffee, and similar plantations worked by slaves brought from Africa. Here, too, were traditions of resistance, not only of the Caribs and other indigenous populations but of the Africans, who mounted small and large uprisings or who ran away from the plantations to establish free "maroon" villages in rain forests or on the mountains.

By the early years of the nineteenth century, two new models had emerged for Caribbean polities. The British in Jamaica and the Dutch in Suriname developed the first during the eighteenth century. They made peace with the warring maroon communities and wrung promises from them to stop attacking the plantations and inciting the slaves to flee. They also set up military units, with manumitted slaves as soldiers under white officers.

Slave revolts continued anyway, but the authorities could hope that they had split the opposition.

The other model was Saint-Domingue, where in 1791 the blacks rose up to push beyond the early reforms of the French Revolution and demand the abolition of slavery. By 1804 the Haitian revolution had been won at the cost of much bloodshed on both sides, the French army had withdrawn from what had once been its most profitable colony, and the ex-slave General Dessalines had been crowned emperor of one of the first societies in which slavery was definitively prohibited.

The Haitian example brought a sharp warning to plantation owners, merchants, and government officials. As Creole elites in the Portuguese and Spanish colonies moved toward revolts for independence in the 1820s, often with conditional support from the blacks, they did not want the Africans to take their own course and fight for the end of slavery. When Great Britain finally abolished slavery in its colonies in 1833, settlers and authorities did not want their former slaves to resist a peaceful and gradual shift to the status of low-paid farm laborers. These hopes were to be dashed by events such as the great Brazilian slave revolt in Bahia in 1835 and the Morant Bay uprising in Jamaica in 1865.

This is the historical world in which Gillo Pontecorvo's *Burn!* (*Queimada*) and Tomás Gutiérrez Alea's *The Last Supper* (*La Última Cena*) are set. Both films were directed by men with strong political commitment who were observing or participating in mid-twentieth-century national revolutions. Yet each film has a beauty and complexity that carry it beyond narrow didacticism. Both films drew from historical research, and Gutiérrez Alea worked closely with an excellent scholar of sugar and slavery. Both films seem to be in cinematic dialogue with Kubrick's *Spartacus*, repeating some of its motifs, yet taking its argument and images in very different directions. The films are different from each other as well, even though both men began their careers under the influence of Italian neorealism. Pontecorvo's *Burn!* was made six years earlier than Gutiérrez Alea's *Last Supper*, so it is best to begin with it and the legacy it left.

ఴఴఴ

Gillo Pontecorvo was born in Pisa in 1919 into an Italian-Jewish family. During World War II he was a Communist partisan and leader of the Resistance in Milan. He said later that his experience of fascism, "the cancer of humanity," and of the war had "shaped [his] idea of the world . . . I am passionate about people and their suffering . . . I felt that I would be able to . . . really communicate these ideas."[1]

His first attempt to communicate after the war was as a journalist in Paris, where he also studied music composition. Then he saw Roberto Rossellini's *Paisan*, the great World War II film made in 1946, which became a founding inspiration for Italian neorealism. He later compared the experience with being struck by lightning. Film became Pontecorvo's medium. After a series of documentaries and films around brief episodes in Italy, he turned to historical films on grand themes: *Kapò* (1959), set in a Nazi concentration camp, *The Battle of Algiers* (1966), and *Burn!* (1969).

To each of these films Pontecorvo brought attitudes and sentiments at creative variance with each other. He had left the Communist party in 1956 in the wake of the Russian invasion of Hungary, but his passion to show "the difficulty of the human condition" grew:

> I have made political films with the idea of creating something powerful that can help to change something else. And I do so because I feel very near to the tragic conditions of people. My compassion is with them, so I have felt a spontaneous urge . . . to tell their stories.[2]

But those stories had to be carefully and thoroughly researched. With Franco Solinas, his regular collaborator on his film scripts, he read and reread books and conducted interviews, all "under the dictatorship of truth." Even then he was not satisfied: described by one of his biographers as having a perfectionist streak, Pontecorvo knew how far he was from grasping the complexity of these historical situations. In his *Battle of Algiers*, for instance, he made a tremendous effort to achieve balance. Pontecorvo's compassion for human suffering would not lead him "to paint black all the action on one side and white on the other." Instead, he would "enter into [different] logics, and see everything that was possible to see." Once he had hoped to be a composer, so it is not surprising that musical themes are very important in his films: they mark and add to the moments of resistance and hope. But for those who listen carefully, there is another tone as well.[3]

In *Burn!*, Pontecorvo said, there were several stories entwined in the same narrative. One was a romance of adventure, in the style of the nineteenth-century English novel (Joseph Conrad's *Nostromo* from 1904 is surely one of the books he had in mind). Another was a confrontation between two sets of ideas: those of the "liberal bourgeoisie" of enterprising England, represented in the person of Sir William Walker; and those of the oppressed of the colonial world, as represented by José Dolores, leader of the black revolts. In all, the film was a fictional parable of linked historical transitions: from slave regime to free labor; from old imperial colony to independent nation dominated by foreign capital. Pontecorvo, together with scriptwriters Solinas and Franco Giorgio Arloria, put together events from Brazil, Saint-Domingue, Jamaica, Cuba, and elsewhere and set them on the imaginary island of Queimada.[4]

℘℘℘

The film opens in the early 1840s as Sir William Walker's boat nears Queimada and the ship's captain explains that *queimada* means "burned" in English. The Portuguese had once set fire to the entire island to put down initial Amerindian opposition to their conquest. Walker is on a clandestine mission from the British Admiralty, with approval from the Royal Antilles Sugar Company, to foment a slave uprising along with a Creole declaration of independence from Portuguese rule. Just as he arrives, Santiago, the current leader of the slaves, is discovered by the authorities and executed. Walker looks about for a new leader and finds him in the young José Dolores, who had carried his valises when he got off the boat. First he taunts Dolores into defiance against himself, then inspires and trains him for resistance against slavery and the Portuguese. The initial step is a bank robbery, followed, as Walker foresees, by an attack on the white soldiers who track down the money, and then by a general slave uprising led by Dolores.

Meanwhile, Walker persuades the Creole elite and plantation owners of the economic advantages of free workers over slaves. He plots with them the assassination of the Portuguese governor. These events come together on a night of slave carnival, at the end of which the new president, Teddy Sanchez, declares the independence of Queimada and, shortly afterward, the abolition of slavery.

Dolores, who is now called General Dolores by the people, comes to town with his armed entourage, wanting to claim a leadership role in the new republic. After a month, with no agreement on a constitution between him and President Sanchez, and with the sugar rotting in the harbor, Dolores returns to his encampment, where the blacks are still in arms and refusing to work on the sugar plantations. Walker has already tried to persuade Dolores that "civilization is not a simple matter. You cannot learn it overnight." Dolores, now very troubled, finally instructs his followers to lay down their arms and go back to the plantations. He warns Walker to tell his white friends that "they may know how to sell sugar, but we are the ones who cut the cane."

Ten years pass. Sir William Walker has been to Indo-China, among other places, and has returned to London "another man," quarrelsome, dissolute, and living in a poor neighborhood. The Royal Antilles Sugar Company has made immense profits from its plantations all over the Caribbean, except in Queimada, where the sugar-cane cutters have been in revolt under General Dolores and have won several victories, despite being outnumbered by the Queimada soldiers. The film resumes the tale as Walker is employed by the Royal Antilles Sugar Company, with support from Her Majesty's government, to put down the revolt. Efforts at negotiation fail when Dolores refuses to see Walker. Walker learns from one of Dolores's followers of the general's revolutionary critique of the white man's civilization: "It is better to know where to go than how to go."

Walker coldly plans military actions, which are carried out by Queimada troops, including many black soldiers, and additional British troops. As black families are herded out of their huts, the mountain villages that give support to the rebels are burned. Before long, most of the other villages and the plantations also go up in flames. Altogether, there is much loss of life. President Sanchez wants to stop the attack, but Walker engineers his arrest by the commander of the Queimada troops, and Sanchez is executed for treason.

When Dolores is finally captured, he refuses to say a word to Walker, but tells the black soldiers who are willing to listen: "One of us will remain. We will be born later." Walker tries to get Dolores to escape, so he will not be executed and become a martyr and a myth. Dolores looks at Walker in silent triumph and shouts as he is led off to be hanged: "Inglese, but what civilization? Till

José Dolores led off to the gallows.

when?" While workers load the cargo of sugar, Walker walks to the boat to return to England. A voice like Dolores's asks if he can carry Walker's bags, and, as Sir William smiles and turns, he is killed with a knife.

ᔕᔕᔕ

Pontecorvo cast Marlon Brando for the role of Sir William Walker, and followed his preferred practice of casting José Dolores and the other black figures from the rural population of Colombia, his initial site for shooting. He saw Evaristo Marquez riding horseback in the countryside one day and decided he was perfect for the leader of the blacks. Marquez's only language was a Spanish-African Creole, and he had to be coached into speaking English, just as José Dolores was coached into making revolution.

Unlike *Spartacus,* Burn! gives some background to slave revolts. Santiago's rebel movement, centered in a mountain village of free blacks, or maroons, has been crushed, but it provides a tradition of resistance on the island. Dolores seems not to know of it, however, or at least not to build on that tradition when he meets Walker, even though Santiago's head has been paraded around the villages as a warning. Walker chooses Dolores when he sees him sneak food to a newly arrived slave mother in chains with her infant, and then throw a stone at a soldier trying to prevent Dolores from doing so.

The path to armed revolt is a double one. Most evidently, the white gentleman, acting for the interests of Britain, the sugar trade, and "progress and civilization," manipulates the black slave porter until he is prepared to kill Portuguese soldiers to be free. This transfer of energy and intention is expressed at critical junctures through the faces of the two men: Sir William looking at Dolores with eyes narrowed in intense expectation; Dolores changing his expression from doubt to certainty, then breaking into a smile.

"If I had told you, José, to start a revolution," Walker says to Dolores after the first victories, "you wouldn't have understood. To rob a bank, yes, that was possible. First you learn to kill to defend yourself. Then . . . to defend others. And the rest came by itself." Dolores goes on to ask Walker, "And you, what do you get?" We film spectators wonder whether the former slave agrees with Walker's patronizing account of how he came to rebel. Enlightenment ideas played a role in the formation of the real Toussaint L'Ouverture's revolutionary sensibility in Saint-Domingue, but they were not bestowed on him by a Frenchman. Rather, Toussaint acquired them from within his own circle on the island. Pontecorvo and Solinas could have learned that from C.L.R. James's *Black Jacobins*, which was available in both French and English when they wrote their film script.[5]

Burn! also shows another path to revolt—that of religion and ceremonial festivity. This route was omitted in *Spartacus*, and

Walker instructing Dolores, who has plans of his own.

it comes into its own in historical scholarship on popular uprising only in the late 1960s. Vodou spirits and Vodou songs of liberty and uprising played their part in preparing, sustaining, and
remembering the Haitian revolution. The leaders of the slave
revolts of 1835 and earlier in Bahia were Afro–Brazilian Muslims,
and the rebels brandished phrases from the Koran along with
their machetes.[6] In *Burn!*, versions of African song and ceremony
burst on the screen at important moments, sometimes mixed
with Christian motifs as well. There is a cross near Santiago's coffin, but his wake is marked by drumming, African chanting, and
dancing. Men, women, and children dance after Dolores's first
victory over the Portuguese, some of them brandishing rifles
and wearing soldiers' hats. The carnival that culminates in the
assassination of the Portuguese governor lasts all day. It is infused
with African motifs, the slaves are brilliantly costumed, their children are covered with white fluid to make them look like ghosts,
and their cries and dances transfix the soldiers until it is time

for the attack. Ennio Morricone's music underscores the same message, and the theme associated with revolt is heard in counterpoint with an African song.

Slave children paint their bodies before the carnival.

The slaves of Queimada in carnival before the revolt.

Sir William Walker is performed with intensity and absorp-
tion by Marlon Brando. He fought ferociously with Pontecorvo
during the film, but has said recently: "I think I did the best
acting I've ever done in that picture."[7] Walker is in many ways
the central figure in *Burn!*, yet his story is always placed against
that of Dolores. Whereas in Kubrick's film, Spartacus and Crassus are opponents throughout, in Pontecorvo's film Walker and
Dolores are collaborators. They are cheerful collaborators in
their first encounters—exchanging Dolores's rum for Walker's
whisky and toasting each other's projects—and enemies in their
last.

Their life trajectories move in opposite directions. Walker
begins with belief in "civilization and progress," in freedom of
sorts along with managing and profit making. He ends in doubt,
commenting with icy accuracy, as he watches the capture of Dolores, on the irony of the English treatment of the black leader.
He says he no longer knows *why* he is in Queimada, but affirms
that he still likes to do things well. Dolores begins in uncertainty,
without a clear plan or a moral and social philosophy. He ends in
belief, challenging the goals of the "white man's civilization,"
which cares only for technical progress, and asserting, "If a man
works for another . . . he remains a slave."

The final conflict between the two men is not just political or
ideological, but personal. Sir William wants to win as a man over
General Dolores. He holds out his hand in vain to the captured
leader. He insults the silent Dolores, who then spits in his face.
Dolores's victory is in their final moments together, when he refuses to escape. Pontecorvo intended this scene to show the cost
of Dolores's martyrdom to Walker himself: "If José is killed . . .
without even speaking one word to him, José would become
greater than Walker, who would then feel as if he had lost everything."[8] In his last words to the silent Dolores, Walker bursts
forth with the question he has abandoned for his own life and

which the rebel leader thinks all important: "Why?" Why does José want to die? Why?

⁄9⁄9⁄9

Burn! is a tough movie, with more balance to it than *Spartacus*. The violence of the Queimada and British forces is horrendous—the burning, the uprooting of population, and the setting of dogs on the rebels (as was done in Saint-Domingue by Napoleon's army in 1802)[9]—but Dolores also teaches, "We must cut heads instead of cane," and refuses negotiation by sending back a wagon of dead men. The ex-slaves are not all brothers: the troops of independent Queimada who hunt down the rebels are mostly black, and some of these black soldiers cruelly mock the captured Dolores.[10] The rulers do not all become as ruthless as Walker, the commanders of the Queimada and British troops, and the agent of the Royal Antilles Sugar Company: the mestizo President Sanchez is a moderate who believes that independence should have brought something better than domination by foreign capital and massive violence, and he pays for it with his life.

Apart from the power of its celebratory and festive scenes and the terror of its scenes of destruction, the historical achievement of *Burn!* is in its successful experiment in telling specific and general stories at the same time. *Burn!* not only suggests how events of the past are experienced by village groups or lived out in the personal rivalry of two men (the microhistorical potential of film) but also tries to give a general account of shifts in power and class and the rhythm of historical change (the iconic potential of film). Pontecorvo once said that his ideal director would be three-quarters Rossellini, the focused storyteller, and one-quarter Eisenstein, the teller of grand sweep.[11]

In *Burn!* this general picture is offered in part by having individual persons stand for a large social process: the British consul to Queimada in the Portuguese period becomes the representative of the Royal Antilles Sugar Company in the period of independence. It is also offered by commentary, as Sir William Walker both performs his strategic and manipulative tasks and, like a chorus, comments on them. At Walker's first meeting with President Sanchez and his colleagues on his return to Queimada, Sir William suddenly pauses and reflects on the interval in which he has been away:

> Very often between one historical period and another ten years might certainly be long enough to reveal the contradictions of a whole century. And so often we have to realize that our judgments and our interpretation and even our hopes may have been wrong—wrong, that's all.

By skillful acting, Marlon Brando is both out of character and in character as he makes this uncolloquial observation; the film audience catches the convention of commentary being displayed and then the slippage of Walker back to his own life, as he lowers his eyes and his voice on the phrase, "even our hopes may have been wrong." Many historians would find Pontecorvo's historical schema oversimplified and would substitute other terms for his Marxist "contradictions," but they would agree that there are time intervals that seem to participants to have a distinctive character and a sense of shift (our own *fin de siècle* seems to be one).

Pontecorvo adds complexity to his narrative not by words, but by images and sounds that close and open the history. There is Dolores's face, caught twice in a still in Walker's telescope: early in the film in anger as he picks up a stone to throw at the Portuguese soldier; at the end as he climbs a mountainside and reaches back to help a fellow rebel. There is the color white: at the opening the white of a big rock off the coast of Queimada, which, the ship's captain recounts, is said to come from the bones of the Africans who had died while crossing the ocean and were cast off there; the white covering of the children at carnival; the whiteness of the ash overlying the mountains of Queimada at the end. Then there are the parallel futures imagined after the burning: in Walker's words to the sugar company man, the destroyed island will be green again after ten years and producing sugar, restored as it had been after the Portuguese burning; in Dolores's words to a sympathetic black soldier: "It is natural that fire destroys everything. A little life always remains. One of us will remain. We will be born later."

In *Spartacus*, the child that survives can be a form of resistance as well as the hope for the future. In *Burn!*, the child—here the boy child—plays both the role of hope and the role of sorrow. During the heady days of early rebel success, when slavery is being destroyed and the island has declared its independence, José Dolores is a charismatic figure: the women and men of the

villages and city streets dance around him with joy. The women in particular hold their little boys up to him, to be touched and held. During the days of burning and the eviction of villagers, the little boys are at the center again, but now alone, baffled, terrified as they run crying in the smoke and gun fire. They are a reproach both to Sir William Walker and to General José Dolores. In Ennio Morricone's music for these scenes, the crying of a little boy cuts through the grand motifs, reminding us of the costs of both rebellion and oppression.

$\wp\wp\wp$

In 1951, about the same time that Gillo Pontecorvo returned to Rome to make his first documentary, a young man named Tomás Gutiérrez Alea arrived there from Cuba to study film at the Centro Sperimentale di Cinematografia. His first film on his return, a neorealist story about workers, was promptly banned by the Batista government. After the Cuban revolution of 1959, Gutiérrez Alea came into his own as a filmmaker: his subjects became more wide-ranging, and his style, influenced by neorealism and the French New Wave, moved in a distinctive direction shared with his Cuban contemporaries. As he put it, "Our film production must of necessity be inexpensive . . . [so it] is a kind of light, agile cinema, directly founded on our own reality . . . But it also succeeds . . . in producing an impact somehow charged with poetry."[12]

For some of his own films, Gutiérrez Alea might have added "charged with humor," as in his 1966 *Death of a Bureaucrat*, a hilarious satire on bureaucracy. His last film before his death, *Guantanamera* (1995), a love story and a poignant tale of loss, was also a spoof on the failures of central economic planning. His *Memories of Underdevelopment* (1968) established him as one of the most important filmmakers in Latin America. Sergio, its thirty-eight-year-old hero, is adrift in the Cuba of the early 1960s, strangely detached from his relatives and friends, who are leaving for the United States, from the women he has affairs with or fantasies about in Havana, and from the revolution around him. Shown through fragmentary flashbacks, Sergio's inner life in some ways anticipates the melancholy of the count in Gutiérrez Alea's *Last Supper*, a film with a very different narrative structure.

The *Last Supper* of 1976 was Gutiérrez Alea's first historical film and his first film in color. In making it, he became part of a group of cinema people and historians who were trying to reconstruct Cuba's past. They were especially interested in slavery and slave activity, which they felt had been ignored or misrepresented in the historical writing of the bourgeois Cuban Republic. Sergio Giral, for example, encouraged by his mentor Gutiérrez Alea, made three important films on slavery, one drawn from Cuba's first abolitionist novel of 1839, another from an oral history of a runaway slave, and a third from a diary kept by a hunter of fugitives.[13] Gutiérrez Alea himself turned for collaboration to Manuel Moreno Fraginals, author of a remarkable book, *The Sugarmill (El Ingenio)*, first published in Havana in 1964.

Moreno Fraginals understood sugar manufacturing and business mentalities: his father had been a sugarmill administrator and technician, and he himself had worked for a decade for different business firms. He had also loved history since his student days, when he wrote about slaves and wage workers in Cuba's past. After the Cuban revolution, he returned full time to history, availing himself of the abundant sugarmill papers and account books newly deposited in the National Library. But archives and old books were not enough for him: he visited folklore centers, interviewed old-timers, and found a traditional sugarmill where he could try out the early techniques.[14]

El Ingenio, when it appeared, was a pioneering reconstruction of the life, procedures, calculations, and struggles of those who owned, managed, and worked at the sugarmills. Translated into English in 1976 as *The Sugarmill*, it won an American Historical Association prize as the best work on Latin American history over a five-year period. Moreno Fraginals concentrated on the

late eighteenth and early nineteenth centuries, when Cuba gradually took over the primacy that Saint-Domingue had once had
in sugar production. It was a time when canefields spread in
many parts of the island; when sugarmills multiplied, allowing
the owners to export processed rather than raw sugar; and when
the number of slaves brought in from Africa each year increased
twentyfold. Among the stories he told, derived from a document
in the archives of the Real Consulado (Royal Council), was that
of the Count de Casa Bayona, who on Maundy Thursday, 1789,
washed the feet of twelve of his black slaves and sat them at his
table in imitation of the Last Supper of Jesus Christ and his Apostles. Instead of being grateful, the men organized a revolt and
burned down the count's sugarmill. Once caught, they were
executed and their heads placed on pikes.[15] This was the tale
recounted on screen in Gutiérrez Alea's *Last Supper*, for which
Moreno Fraginals, himself experienced in film and television,
served as consultant.

ʚᵹʚᵹʚᵹ

The film compresses these happenings into the five days of Holy
Week—they actually occurred from Palm Sunday to Easter Sunday[16]—and dates them "in the last years of the eighteenth century." This imprecision was to reset the events to take place after,
rather than before, the revolution in Saint-Domingue. The story
opens on Holy Wednesday as the ferocious overseer, Don
Manuel, sends his aides and dogs out to pursue Sebastián, a recalcitrant slave on his third escape. The count arrives from his residence in Havana at his sugarmill, where he greets his overseer,
his priest, his technician-refiner, and his house slaves. He talks
with his priest, who assures him that everything is planned for
the dinner the next evening, tells him how difficult it is to teach
Christian truth to the blacks, but complains about the cruelty of

Don Manuel to the slaves and his unwillingness to let them take time off from work to attend mass. The count informs the overseer that he must respect the commands of the church. When Don Manuel responds that he must whip the slaves and put them in stocks to get enough sugar cane cut, the count shrugs: "Why tell me? You're the overseer."

The count visits the workshop of the technician Gaspar Duclé, an articulate and independent-minded mulatto from Saint-Domingue. Duclé is full of plans for improving the furnace and the grinding mill, but he warns the count that he will require more slave labor. "Don't worry," the count replies, delighted with Duclé's ideas, "we know how to handle blacks." Just then the runaway Sebastián is brought back and whipped. Don Manuel viciously cuts off his ear. The count gags, but does nothing to intervene.

The next day, Maundy Thursday, the count has Don Manuel choose twelve men from among the slaves, requesting that Sebastián, with his bloody bandage around his head, be among them. The priest prepares them for the service, describing the scene in heaven where they will sit at the Lord's table, but reminding them that here they must serve and love the master. The count washes and kisses the slaves' feet in the church; some of them laugh in astonishment. The dinner follows in a beautiful candlelit room, which is filmed in a soft ochre color. The table is laden with food, and the diners are disposed around the count as in the great religious paintings of the sixteenth and seventeenth centuries. The count tells his guests that, at his last meal, Christ called together "the saints, his disciples, who were his slaves." Some of the blacks say who they are and what work they do, and two of them ask favors of the master, including old Pascual, who is granted freedom from his final year of servitude. But Sebastián, summoned by the count to sit on his right, refuses to speak, and when the count shouts, "Who am I . . . I ask you in the name of

The count's last supper.

Christ, who am I?" Sebastián spits at him (see page 2). After a long
silence, the count wipes his face and says that, like Christ, who
was spat at and stoned, he can humble himself before his slaves.

Four stories are recounted around the table. One is an explanation of "why blacks cry," told, sung, and danced with ironic
laughter by a slave from West Africa. He tells of a family back
home, where a father tearfully plans to sell his favorite son to the
whites because his kinfolk have no food. When the son succeeds
in selling his father first, he is punished when he brings back the
food. His punishment is being sold into slavery. "So the family
ate twice . . . The blacks are crying . . . If you're not a black slave,
you don't know why."[17]

Two more stories are told with lively drama by the count:
one a story of Saint Francis and Brother Leo, which culminates
in the teaching that the greatest happiness is in patiently bearing
the suffering sent by God; the other the story of the loss of Paradise through the disobedience of Eve and Adam, and the possibility of Paradise after death through sacrifice. All these tales are
greeted with laughter and some discussion about "no master, no

slave, and no overseer" in Paradise. The count, full of wine, drifts off to sleep in joy, feeling that it is good to share with his slaves, that there is no Judas among them, that the wall of hatred falls if each knows his role.

Now Sebastián breaks his silence to tell a Yoruba creation story of the high god Olofin, who made Truth beautiful and Lies ugly, but gave the puny Lies a machete in compensation. Lies cut off Truth's head, and Truth, reaching blindly about, pulled off Lies's head and put it on her body. Sebastián puts a pig's head from the platter in front of his face and says, "Since then Truth has travelled the world deceiving all people."[18]

He and the other slaves debate the count's promise that they need not work on Good Friday. The singer dances about chanting merrily, "Black man won't work, Slave will rest." Sebastián is emphatic that he will not work and adds that he has special powers: "No one can catch me, no one can kill me." He blows powder from his pouch on the count's face, who awakens, startled, and leaves.

In the morning, the count departs early for Havana. Don Manuel rings the work bell and whips the slaves out, for there are quotas to meet. The priest tries unsuccessfully to get him to stop, then rides to the city to tell the count. Although the count agrees that the slaves should not work on Good Friday, he will not interfere: the mill is the "overseer's world." Meanwhile, Sebastián has led the slaves in an uprising, killing one of the overseer's men and putting Don Manuel in the same wooden stocks in which he punishes slaves.

Notified of the uprising, the count is enraged, mutters about Saint-Domingue, and rides back with troops to put it down. Warned of his approach, Sebastián kills Don Manuel and, together with the other slaves, puts the sugarmill to the torch, sparing only

the church and Duclé's house. On his arrival, the count associates Don Manuel's death with the death of Christ on Good Friday. He orders his men to seek out the treacherous twelve slaves who had supped with him and to mount their heads on posts.

The camera follows these "disciples" as they are pursued ferociously by dogs and men, and die in various ways. Only Sebastián has escaped, protected from capture by the technician Duclé, who now departs himself from the sugarmill. On Easter Sunday, eleven heads are impaled on posts around the grounds. The count announces that he will build a new church in memory of Don Manuel, and he orders three slaves to erect a cross on the spot where the overseer had been slain. His sugarmill will rise again, he promises. The film ends with shots of Sebastián running free in the mountains, images of a flying bird and falling water, and the sound of an African song underscoring his invincibility.

☙☙☙

The Last Supper is a cinematic microhistory that is tightly linked to evidence from the Cuban past. Not only does it show different types of grinding mills, residence habits of plantation owners, male to female ratios among slaves, wooden stocks and other practices of punishment but it documents the conflict between the devotional practice urged by priests and the Spanish government, on the one hand, and the production schedules urged by administrators, on the other. The episode itself occurred not long before the proclamation of the Spanish Royal Code of 1789 "on the education, treatment, and employment of the slaves in all [the king's] dominions," known in Cuba as the Codigo Negro (Black Code). Among other provisions, the code required the religious instruction of slaves and the observance of feast days, during which the slaves were not to be obliged to work, and limited punishment to twenty-five lashes, which could not cause bleeding. Sugarmill owners indignantly protested against the code. As evidence that the religious provisions would not work, they recounted the ritual and revolt on the estate of the pious Count de Casa Bayona.[19]

Moreno Fraginals could cite these materials as well as diocesan pronouncements, priests' tracts, sugarmill owners' letters, and government interventions documenting issues that, in the film, are narrated economically and simply. This underpinning is not only gratifying to the historian's sense of veracity but also engenders a concrete richness in the film. It creates a more believable and distinctive world for spectators.[20]

Beyond believable concreteness, *The Last Supper* brings multiplicity to the past in its representation of social types. For the count and his three associates, some complexity of character is introduced. The associates are not drawn from actual persons, whose names were not given in the account of the episode, but are composites of figures found on every sugarmill. Don Manuel is the simplest: he is brutal, he drinks and preys on the slave women even though he has a wife, he is disgusted by the count's religiosity—stamping out of the church during the feet-washing—and he thinks only of production. He is the stereotypical cruel overseer, of which some existed; his actions in the film are precisely those prohibited in the code of 1789. The priest has more range: he teaches the slaves obedience and patience along with Christian doctrine, as the Catholic manuals of his time encouraged, but he tries in his timid way to persuade the count to limit the overseer's violence and to allow the slaves their holy days for prayers. Duclé, with his expertise in sugar refining, enthusiasm for improvement, and enlightened secularism—he does not attend the Maundy Thursday service—was clearly an attractive figure for these Cuban artists and intellectuals in the 1970s: as an example of the best "progressive" element of the "new bourgeoisie," he also rises beyond narrow class interest. A mulatto fearful of what black domination brought in Saint-Domingue— "I don't want to see my head used by the blacks as a football," he said to the overseer—Duclé nonetheless does not beat the slaves in his refinery, conceals Sebastián's presence from his hunters, at risk to himself, and departs from the sugarmill at the height of the executions.[21]

The count was described as "humane, kind, and religious" by his fellow sugarmill owners in 1790, and as "an example of religious hypocrisy" by the reviewers of *The Last Supper* and by

Gutiérrez Alea himself.[22] He is a more complicated figure in the film than in either of these descriptions. Resembling Sergio in *Memories of Underdevelopment*, the count is torn between an older time, when Cuban plantations and sugarmills were named after saints, and a newer one, when the names are being changed to Friendship, Hope, Chance, and the like. He says he is "unwell," "uneasy," "in a maze of darkness," and "tired," and seeks solace by contemplating the crucified Christ. His solution is not so much hypocrisy as compartmentalization and an attitude of laissez-faire. The priest, the technician, and the overseer each play their role, and if the overseer sins by excess—well, God will punish him in the next world. For the count, the feet washing and the dinner with his slaves bring him humility and "joy," as he believes for a few hours that there is harmony between master and slaves.

The count is transformed when he learns of the revolt and then takes decisive action. He no longer needs the dead Manuel to order punishment; he orders it himself. He no longer depends on the priest to advise him on religion; he tells the priest that no rebel slaves can be blessed within the church and that their heads must be on pikes. Shouting his commands before his burned sugarmill, the count tears off the powdered wig he has worn up till then and reveals his middle-aged head of hair. This gesture does not signify that the "real" count has appeared from under a hypocritical exterior; rather, he has been changed—and for the worse—in the view of the departing technician.

The count is still a problematical figure, and there might have been a more nuanced treatment of his shift. With the slaves, however, the accomplishment of *The Last Supper* is considerable, as individual persons emerge with their own traits well beyond anything seen in *Spartacus* or *Burn!*. Here, as with the overseer, the priest, and the technician, the characters are created out of extensive information about the origins and behavior of slaves on many plantations.[23] Most of the twelve men at the Holy Thursday dinner say something during the meal. Most are born in Africa, and two in Cuba. Gutiérrez Alea decided that all of them would be able to understand Spanish—an unlikely situation that was needed for the dynamic of the dinner—but there is a suggestion of the Creole language current among the *bozales* (newcomers from Africa) and their fellow slaves in the doubled verbs used in the singer's story: "walk-walk," "cry-cry." The contrasts among men from different African regions is suggested, but all the dinner guests listen attentively to Sebastián's Yoruba tale, which, presumably, was suggested by Rogelio Martínez Furé, the consultant on African matters for the film.[24]

What is striking are the different personalities and claims of the men around the table. The light-skinned Antonio, a Christian who wants to believe that the master is good, yearns to be back in the house away from the "dirty slaves" in the cane fields, to which the overseer has nastily banished him. Poised and fearless Bongaché, a king in his native Guinea and himself once a seller of war captives into slavery, now works in the refinery and will lead the revolt with Sebastián. Old, worn Pascual, when he wins his freedom, tearfully says he has no place to go. The expressive singer and dancer will later die by believing, as the Congo custom taught, that he is sprouting wings and can fly like a bird to escape Don Manuel's dogs.[25] And the proud and stubborn Sebastián, a dignified teller of important tales, announces to his fellows that he has special powers, as he shows them his pouch of powder. He has had his ear cut off, a humiliating mutilation known well from the African-Cuban tale of the river goddess Oba, but he is not cowed.[26] He is a man of strength and a man of African magic, an inspiration to the slaves and a Judas to the count.

The revolt on Good Friday—and it actually happened on Good Friday[27]—grows out of the events on Holy Thursday. It is one of the historical gifts of this film to depict how resistance is aroused and legitimated by the crossing of two cultural forms. In this regard, *The Last Supper* goes beyond the gladiator fights of *Spartacus* and the juxtaposition of ideas and festive ceremonial in *Burn!* to the transformation of thoughts and feelings in the very course of ceremonial experience. Here, picturing can surpass prose in showing how a change takes place.

The washing of feet on Maundy Thursday and the Last Supper as reenacted by the count are both examples of "rites of inversion"—of the world turned upside down. High becomes low, and low becomes high; boundaries of social and political hierarchy are temporarily effaced. For some, the topsy-turvy experience is blowing off steam, to be followed by a return to normal order. But for others, the reversal can flow over into regular life, as the memory of liminal openness changes expectations.[28] Both of these consequences emerge from the count's dinner, partly because his guests had something of their own to say along the way.

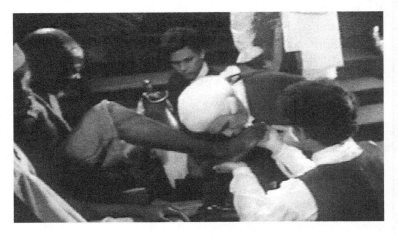

Washing the feet of the poor in church on Holy Thursday had long been a practice of European monarchs, including the Spanish king, and of bishops in the Old World and the New. The historical Count of Casa Bayona would presumably have seen it performed by the bishop in the diocese of Cuba, but performing it himself on his own slaves and having them to dinner in the role of the apostles was, in Moreno Fraginals's words, "out of the question" among plantation owners in Cuba. "This was an eccentric initiative of the count."[29] In the film, the count moves through the ritual process, accepting the humiliation of being spat upon by Sebastián, moving gradually to a state of ease as he shares food and tells his disciples his message of suffering, and ending in a state of joy after describing Paradise. "This and nothing else is Paradise," he says as he falls drunkenly asleep.

The dinner guests have also changed during the ritual process, from the early embarrassed and even frightened laughter at the outlandish washing of their feet to a more expansive and somewhat irreverent laughter as they eat, drink, and hear stories. They have seen the master accept the insult from Sebastián and have heard him grant old Pascual his freedom; they have asked questions about the count's Christian tales—"You mean if the overseer beats me, I should be happy?"—and have offered their own views: "I'll take Paradise. It's better." They have got the inside message from the singer's songs ("the blacks are crying . . . If you're not a black slave, you don't know why"), have listened quietly to Sebastián's cautionary Yoruba tale about Lies abroad in the world, and have seen signs of his powers. The slave-apostles fall asleep at the table as they talk about not working tomorrow.

On Good Friday, the world is turned right side up again for the count, and the slaves should have learned the lesson of patience. For the slaves, the world must be kept upside down, the overseer must be overthrown, and, as the priest warns the count, the master should learn the lesson of justice.

Gutiérrez Alea changed the historical denouement of the revolt from twelve heads on the pike to eleven. This is at least a plausible shift, for there were numerous maroon communities (*palenques*) of escaped slaves in remote parts of the mountains in

Cuba at that time. Instead of a child surviving the lost battle, as in *Spartacus* and *Burn!*, it is here the leader, Sebastián. This twist is in part a recognition of the gross imbalance between male and female rural slaves in the last half of the eighteenth century in Cuba—it would shift only in the nineteenth century—and few slave women and no children are seen in the film at the count's sugarmill.[30] In addition, Sebastián's invincibility reflects the African–American folktale tradition of metamorphosis: "Sebastián will become a tree, a fish, a stone, he'll turn himself into a bird and fly away," he has assured his fellow diners. "No one can catch me, no one can kill me." And his story lives on in the film.

4

Witnesses of Trauma:
Amistad *and* Beloved

THE SINGER'S TALE in *The Last Supper*—of famished Africans selling family members into slavery—is a story of trauma, an inner secret of "why blacks cry." Stories of this kind circulated in West Africa, the southern United States, and the Caribbean, often with Hare and Hyena or Rabbit and Wolf as the hungry sellers and their mothers as the victims. One seller (Hare or Rabbit) secretly cuts the cord so his mother can escape, but food is still provided by the sale of the other mother.[1] These are tales that bring bitter laughter and leave a wound.

Two films in particular portray trauma and the memory of trauma, one as a partial strand, the other at its heart. *Amistad* and *Beloved* both deal with unspeakable violence, perpetrated on African people by others or sometimes by other Africans, and investigate the crossover between violence and resistance. Both look at the cost of enslavement to family life, and the struggle, fraught with ghosts and guilt, for family continuity. Unlike *Spartacus*, which was made amid the troubles of the Cold War and the Red Scare, or *Burn!* and *The Last Supper*, which were produced in the wake of national revolutions, *Amistad* and *Beloved* were composed under the shadow of Holocaust.

The initial seizure of persons in Africa for enslavement and the terrors of the voyage, or Middle Passage, from West Africa to the Antilles are both documented in history books. Until recently, however, as Toni Morrison has suggested, these episodes have played only a small role in the popular memory of African Americans.[2] True, they have been the stuff of novels: Alhafi Sir Abubakar Tafawa Balewa's *Shaihu Umar* describes the seizure of slaves within Hausa society itself; and Olumide, in Caryl Phillips's *Cambridge*, recalls his seizure and transport from Guinea. They have also been the subject of poetry: in Book 3 of Derek Walcott's *Omeros*, the boat of the fisherman Achille is pulled back to his "home" by a sea-swift; later, in his African village, he relives the archers' raid, "the flung arc of the net," watches "the chain of men linked by their wrists" being marched away, and faints as he thinks of them "arriving at the sea's rim . . . and entering inside the dark hold."[3]

Still, the details of such events have not been central in the abundant literature of African-American memoirs, stories, and songs. In folk tales and songs, echoes of the initial violent seizure and the Middle Passage are infrequent: the hungry family selling its members is an unusual theme.[4] In memoirs, the most graphic portrait of these episodes is one of the earliest. In the 1789 *Interesting Narrative: The Life of Olaudah Equiano*, the former slave described the crossing: the "stench," "the galling of the chains," the "filth," "the shrieks of the women, and the groans of the dying." But Nancy Prince, born free in Massachusetts in 1799, was spared the violent particulars by her grandfather and stepfather, or at least she spared the readers of her 1850 *Narrative*, where she elaborated rather on escape:

[My grandfather] often used to tell us, when little children, the evils of Slavery, and how he was stolen from his native land . . . My stepfather was stolen from Africa, and while the vessel was at anchor in one of our Eastern ports, he succeeded in making his escape from his captors by swimming ashore . . . There were two of them . . . I have often heard him describe the beautiful moonlight night when they two launched their bodies into the deep, for liberty.

Jacob Stroyer, born in South Carolina in 1849, was briefer still: "My father was born in Sierra Leone, Africa. Of his parents and his brothers and sisters I know nothing. I only remember that it was said that his father's name was Monocosa, and his mother's Mongomo."[5]

In the narratives of ex-slaves collected in 1936–38 by the Federal Writers' Project, the speakers with parents or grandparents born in Africa will sometimes tell how they were "stolen" or tricked on board boat, but details on the Middle Passage are sparse. The fullest descriptions sound like those given by Phillip Evans, who had been a slave in South Carolina: "My pappy often tell mammy and us chillun, dat his pappy was ketched in Africa and fetched to America on a big ship in a iron cage, 'long wid a whole heap of other black folks, and dat he was powerful sick at de stomach de time he was on de ship." Similarly, Josephine Howard, who had been a slave in Alabama, recounted: "My mammy and her mammy gits took out to dat big boat and dey locks dem in a black hole what mammy say so black you don't see nothin'."[6]

In contrast, slave memoirs frequently recall the distress of being sold in the American South and the cruelty, whippings, and harassment of overseers, masters, and mistresses. Occasionally, too, there are accounts of kindness. Perhaps it is the pursuit of "roots" among African Americans in recent years that has allowed these traumas to be looked at more steadily and fully. The Elmina Castle in Ghana, through whose dungeons hundreds of thousands of Africans passed into slavery, is now a much visited site. After the guides have led a reenactment of imprisonment, everyone joins in singing "We Shall Overcome" and African songs.[7]

Whatever the case here, it was the revolt of the Africans on the *Amistad* and the heroism of Joseph Cinqué that first aroused the passion of the black actor Debbie Allen.

≡≡≡

In 1978 Debbie Allen read a book about the *Amistad* and was "stunned, overjoyed, proud, outraged, and in tears." What a story: Africans seized in 1839 and transported illegally across the Atlantic; a mutiny, led by Cinqué (Sengbe Pieh, to give his original Mende name) off the coast of Cuba; seizure of the Africans; and a celebrated set of trials in the United States that led to the Africans being declared free persons. Many slave ships crossed the ocean each year in violation of the Spanish-English treaty of 1820 prohibiting that trade, but only a few had a successful revolt of their "cargo." One other slaver had been the source of a trial in the United States—the Spanish *Antelope* in 1825—but it had not become a *cause célèbre* like the *Amistad*, with abolitionists, the Spanish queen, and the American president all involved. For Allen, who had marched with her parents in the civil rights movement, it was important that the book recounted "a true story" of African people acting to change their fate, a story she had never heard in school. Now she wanted to make it known to millions of viewers.[8]

Allen built up a research collection on Cinqué and the *Amistad* over the years of her career as an actor and a producer, and finally, in 1994, after seeing *Schindler's List* about the Holocaust, she approached the director, Steven Spielberg. "From the moment I heard of him," Spielberg explains, "Cinqué took up residence in my mind." He, too, had a personal interest in the account, for he had two adopted African Americans among his seven children. "I am making this film for my black children and my white children. They all need to know this story."9

Both Allen and Spielberg had some investment in telling "a true story," as they put it, in making the film "mirror as closely as possible the context in which the story occurred, as well as the actual events as they unfolded." To this end, they used history books, court records, and newspapers, and talked to scholars. David Franzoni, the scenarist, read articles about the Mende people, the community into which Cinqué and a number of the other *Amistad* Africans were born. Arthur Abraham, a distinguished historian of the Mende and Sierre Leone, was summoned from Freetown to consult on the film and to teach the Mende language to those playing the African roles.10 All these actors were West Africans themselves, some still living in their native lands, others (like Djimon Hounsou, who played Cinqué) living in Europe or America. Spielberg told them it was "very good to bring their own experiences into the story," but Hounsou had a better response to his role as actor in events of 160 years before: "There was no experience in my life that I could draw on to play this part . . . My life . . . doesn't come anywhere close to the pain that they suffered on the *Amistad*. If I used what I had gone through in Paris, I would be limiting myself to my own emotions."

Finally, the filmmakers had certain interpretive criteria that affected the historical content of the film and the "look" of the past. The story was to be told as much as possible from the vantage point of Cinqué and the Africans: their view of America and of the people who came to deal with them; their actions in regard to their struggle for freedom. In addition (and perhaps in tension with that other goal), *Amistad* was to "allow for a dramatic rendition that would work as a film for contemporary audiences." As for the cinematic techniques, the director of photography, Janusz Kaminski, wanted to make sure that the images were not too beautiful: "With a period film, it's easy to create sentimental images that will make people say, 'This is so beautiful,' but this story does not call for that kind of approach." Rather, he used a special photographic process that increased the contrast between dark and light and drained away the color. Similarly, Spielberg cut down on energetic camera movements, such as moving it on tracks or a dolly; he wanted viewers to feel they were observing the action in a tableau, rather than being plunged right into it. "I didn't want to bring modern times—which I would equate with long, slick dolly shots—into the nineteenth century," he explained.[11] How does *Amistad* recount the past, especially in regard to the past of its African characters?

The film opens with an intense closeup of Cinqué's face as he desperately picks a spike from a post with his bloody fingers and uses it to remove his chains. Successful, he and other freed men take cane cutters from the cargo and revolt in the midst of a ferocious storm. Cinqué, with some dread on his face, kills the captain while others kill the cook. Using sign language, Cinqué orders their two Cuban purchasers, Jose Ruiz and Pedro Montez, to take them east to Africa, but as the weeks pass, he and a companion realize from the night sky that they are being deceived. Nearing the American shore to get water, the *Amistad* is seized by an American naval vessel. The Africans—four children and forty men—are taken in chains to a New Haven prison, where they shout and weep as the prison doors close upon them.

The film then alternates scenes in which the different parties who will be active in the case express their interest: the girl queen of Spain, Isabella, who claims that the Africans are Cuban slaves on a Spanish ship and belong to Spain; President Van Buren, who is thinking only of his re-election and how not to lose southern support; the abolitionists—the white Lewis Tappan and the black Theodore Joadson—who are sure the Africans are not plantation slaves and vow to help them win their freedom, thereby furthering their cause of ending slavery; and the former president and congressman John Quincy Adams, who at first refuses to be involved in the case.

The main story line moves between the New Haven court and the prison. At the first hearing, at which the Africans are present in chains, competing claims to the ownership of the Africans are stated by the U.S. secretary of state, together with the Spanish ambassador, representing Queen Isabella; the commanders of the American naval vessel; and Ruiz and Montez. The Connecticut district attorney, however, wants to try them, for piracy and murder. Roger Baldwin, a young, somewhat down-and-out real-estate lawyer, offers his services to the abolitionists, saying he will argue the case in terms of property issues, not opposition to slavery: the Africans are not from Cuban plantations, but have been illegally seized and transported. Consequently, they are free persons. When John Quincy Adams refuses Tappan's and Joadson's request for assistance, the abolitionists turn to Baldwin.

Baldwin meets with Cinqué to confirm this account of the prisoners' origins, but even with the help of a Yale linguistics professor, he cannot make himself understood. In a second meeting, by drawing on the ground, he establishes communication with Cinqué, who lets Baldwin know by walking to the end of the prison yard that he comes from very far away. Baldwin and Joadson visit the *Amistad* and discover the hidden cargo list of the *Teçora*, the Portuguese slaver that had taken the Africans across the Atlantic. Meanwhile, Cinqué and his companions talk among themselves in Mende about Baldwin ("He reminds me of that Fula . . . who hires himself out to scrape elephant dung." "A dung scraper might be just the kind of man we need now"). They are also mystified by the evangelical abolitionists who solemnly sing hymns before their prison ("Why do they look so miserable?"). In two hearings before Judge Juttson, as he is called in the film, Baldwin presents what evidence he has—showing, for instance, that the Africans know no Spanish and submitting the *Teçora* list as proof that they were on the slaver—and the judge opines that the men could not be from Cuba.

At this point President Van Buren, pressured by Spain and worried about the southerners, interrupts the proceedings and has Juttson replaced by a young judge from a Catholic family, Judge Coglin, who his advisers believe will make a more opportune decision. Advised by John Quincy Adams that they must get a real "story" from Cinqué, Baldwin and Joadson finally locate a young man from Mende country, Richard Covey, an ex-slave now in the British navy, who can serve as their translator.

A long scene ensues, the heart of the film, with Cinqué, Covey, Baldwin, and Joadson. Baldwin tries to persuade Cinqué to speak at court, saying he has heard he was celebrated by the Mende for killing a lion with a rock. Cinqué tells what happened, but says, "I'm not a big man, just a lucky one." Baldwin reminds him of his leadership in the mutiny, which was more than luck, and Cinqué comments: "That wasn't bravery. Any man would do the same to get back to his family." Joadson gives Cinqué a small animal tusk he has found on the *Amistad*: it had been given to Cinqué by his wife to keep him safe. Then Cinqué tells the story of his departure from his village, all of it shown in a flashback: his capture; his imprisonment with hundreds of others at the dreaded Lomboko fortress, with its African guards and Spanish and Portuguese agents; the ghastly and degrading experience in the hold and on the decks of the *Teçora*; the arrival in

Cuba and the sale of his group at the slave market; the boarding of the *Amistad* and the revolt.

The flashback ceases and the film continues in the courtroom, where Cinqué has been telling the same account through Covey. "I wanted to kill them, too," Cinqué adds, pointing to Ruiz and Montez, "but they convinced some of us they would take us back home." The district attorney tries to undermine Cinqué's testimony, but his story is supported by testimony from a British naval officer who had patrolled the Ivory Coast in search of illegal slave ships.[12] Cinqué suddenly shouts in English, "Give us free! Give us free!" and the chant is taken up by the other men in chains.

Waiting for the verdict back at the prison, Cinqué's companion shows him a Bible, given him by a Christian abolitionist, and tells him the story of Christ through his deciphering of the pictures. At the same time, the camera reveals Judge Coglin praying at a Catholic church. The next day the judge pronounces in favor of the Africans, who were born free and kidnapped, and orders their return to Africa. He also orders the arrest of Ruiz and Mendez for illegal slave trading.

Pressured by both the Spanish ambassador and the southern leader John Calhoun, who speaks of the threat of civil war, Van Buren appeals Coglin's decision to the Supreme Court. At the news, Tappan muses to Joadson that perhaps the martyrdom of the Africans—executed for murder and mutiny on board the *Amistad*—might be more useful to the abolitionist cause than their being freed for rightful self-defense of their liberty. Joadson demurs, and they part somewhat out of sympathy.

Baldwin takes the news to Cinqué, in the midst of joyous celebration in the prison yard. Cinqué is despondent at the turn of events and refuses to speak to him. Baldwin then solicits the aid of John Quincy Adams. This time Adams agrees to work actively on the case, visits the prison in New Haven, and arranges for

Cinqué to be brought to his house. Cinqué suggests questions about the case to Adams, via Covey, and Adams and the Mende leader have a long interview, which opens with their both looking at Adams's African violet. Told by Adams of the difficulties they face—"all we have on our side is a rock," he says, alluding to the lion story, "and our righteousness"—Cinqué responds that he has his ancestors, whom he is calling to him for help. "And they must come, for at this moment I am the whole reason they have existed at all."

The camera moves to the Supreme Court, where Adams presents the final argument for the *Amistad* Africans while Cinqué sits in attendance. Adams begins with critical reference to the "long powerful arm of the executive office" interfering with the work of the American courts. Then he talks of the rightful efforts of the Africans to regain their freedom, "to break loose their chains and try against all odds and prejudices to get home." Because of such acts, he says, Cinqué should be a hero, his story as well known to schoolchildren as that of Patrick Henry, the American Revolutionary leader who had shouted, "Give me liberty or give me death." He reminds the court of the message of the Declaration of Independence that all men are created equal, and comments that as Cinqué and the Mende invoke their ancestors to come to their aid, so those in the courtroom should seek the guidance of their American ancestors. Adams gestures to the busts of past presidents, including his own father, and intones their names. "Who we are is who we were."

The court rules in favor of the freedom of the Africans: the Africans are "free individuals with certain legal and moral rights, including the right to engage in insurrection against those who would deny them their freedom." Cinqué has a moving adieu with Joadson, to whom he gives his little tusk "to keep him safe," and with Baldwin. The last scenes show the British liberating slaves from the fortress of Lomboko and blowing it up, and

Cinqué and the other Africans returning on a boat to Africa, the missionaries standing in the stern. A legend on the screen reports that he found his people engaged in civil war and his village destroyed.

≡≡≡

Viewers would come away from *Amistad* with a general sense of the movement of events, the interests at stake, the arguments being offered and challenged, and the popular excitement and missionary zeal stimulated by the Africans. As a detailed description of the past, however, *Amistad* is not the "mirror . . . [of] actual events as they unfolded," which Spielberg and Allen said they planned. Persons are changed, judicial sentences recast, and times and meetings shifted. Some of this fictionalizing adds interesting depth to the film. Theodore Joadson, as the filmmakers have said, is a composite character, drawn from actual black abolitionists. Lewis Tappan's immediate associates on the *Amistad* Committee were two whites, Rev. Simeon Jocelyn and Rev. Joshua Leavitt, editor of the *Emancipator.* He did, however, collaborate with James Pennington, a black Congregational minister of Connecticut, to raise money for the return of the Africans to their homes and to establish antislavery missions in both the United States and Africa. Joadson's presence allows some remarkable exchanges to occur, and he is a concise reminder of the important role of African-American abolitionists such as Pennington. Unfortunately, the filmmakers could not think of a way to convey Tappan's ceaseless activity.[13]

Some of the fabrication, perhaps intended to increase suspense or character development in the film, seems arbitrary and unnecessary. Roger Baldwin was not an unknown young property lawyer, but a forty-six-year-old defender of fugitive slaves and black education. He came into the *Amistad* case swinging from the start: "All beings, who have form of our nature, are free," he announced at the opening of the first trial, under a Judge Thompson in the circuit court, and was praised for his "masterly speech" by the black abolitionist newspaper *The Colored American*. When that trial ended with a mixed outcome, the case automatically went to a higher court. Van Buren did not punitively change the judge, though he surely was expecting a verdict favoring Spain from district-court Judge Judson.[14] (Presumably to indicate these alterations of the evidence, the judges in the first and second trials in *Amistad* have different names from the actual judges.) As for John Quincy Adams, he was sending informal advice to the Africans' lawyers almost from the start, rather than having to be courted and coaxed.[15]

These changes in the historical record left space in the film for dramatic turns in plot and character. Presumably the refashioning of Baldwin was to develop a "microhistory" out of the relation between Cinqué and Baldwin, as was the case between José Dolores and William Walker in *Burn!*. But in so well-documented a story (compare *Spartacus*), the filmmakers could surely have found drama and microhistorical movement in the events that did occur.

One other set of episodes has drawn fire from historians: the meeting of Cinqué and Adams and the incorporation of some of Cinqué's sentiments into Adams's speech to the Supreme Court. Adams did meet Cinqué in November 1840. After he had agreed, despite his age and health, to be a formal part of the defense team before the Supreme Court, he "visited the prisoners" in Westville prison just outside New Haven. "Cinque and Grabow [sic], the two chief conspirators, have very remarkable countenances," he wrote in his diary.[16] There is no mention of a conversation, however, then or later. Cinqué's influence on Adams through direct discussion was imagined by the filmmakers as a way to show the active role of the Africans in changing their destiny. Like the invention of Joadson, the interchange between the two has a useful symbolic function in the film. It might, however, have been better filled by a more historically plausible construction.

≡≡≡

The historical strength of *Amistad* is in its portrayal of the Africans, and most strikingly in its representation of the seizure of Cinqué, the Middle Passage, and the revolt.

The mere presence of these men in a Connecticut prison in 1839 led *The Colored American* to talk of the Middle Passage: "These unhappy persons are thrust into the hold of a slave ship—treated with a cruelty never inflicted on beasts—suffer all the indescribable horrors of the *Middle Passage*—and at length are landed upon an unknown shore, far from their country, their children, and their homes."[17] Steven Spielberg's gifts in filming extraordinary action, along with those of his director of photography, Janusz Kaminski, who had worked with him on *Schindler's List*, are put to work to give image to these "indescribable horrors." Film viewers are prepared for Cinqué's recital by the earlier visit to the *Amistad* of the abolitionist Theodore Joadson, whose ancestors had come over on such a voyage. Joadson descends into the hold, where chains are swinging everywhere, and falls down in panic as his lantern goes out. Baldwin comes to his aid, but Joadson does not speak about his feelings.

When Cinqué begins his recollection, he is seen in flashback in his Mende village, in brilliant sunlight, his wife smiling and walking with their child. The vision is abruptly broken as African men throw a net around Cinqué and brutally pull him away, even as he offers to share his harvest with them if they set him free. He is taken to Lomboko and then, with many others, placed on the *Teçora*. The Portuguese keepers whip them into the dark

hold, where they are thrown to the floor—men, women, and children naked and weeping—and chained next to each other in rows. Then come the sights and sounds of the passage, a bringing to life of what the slave Olaudah Equiano had put in writing. People are sick and in terror in the storms, babies scream, the dead lie next to the living until they are thrown overboard. On deck, chained men are beaten without mercy, and a woman slips overboard to die with her child. In the stinking hold, where a little rice is slapped into reaching hands, the hungry vie for food and lick it from each other's faces. Most terrible is the drowning of screaming men and women, when the crew decides provisions are running out and the "cargo" must be reduced. The camera follows the bodies into the water, so film viewers will never forget. The *Teçora* arrives at Havana, and a smaller group of Africans are washed, sold, and taken to the *Amistad*. Cinqué frees himself from his chains, and the revolt begins.

The African actors wept and were angry as they played these scenes, and the film crew broke down as well.[18]

In the film, Cinqué could not tell this story to Baldwin and Joadson earlier. The Mende translator, Covey, who in fact had been available at Baldwin's first interview with Cinqué,[19] is not found until the second trial. In addition, Cinqué does not trust Baldwin and Joadson enough to tell strangers such a tale, and they themselves may be unable to listen until after they have seen the *Amistad*. Their faces are not shown after Cinqué's recital, for the scene has switched from the prison to the courtroom, where he is repeating it. When Cinqué actually gave this testimony in January 1840, the newspapers reported that the audience listened in "breathless attention."[20] In the film, the courtroom is quieted by his account.

The district attorney rises to challenge its truth by reminding Cinqué that there is slavery in Africa and that it would be unprofitable and irrational to kill slaves the way he has alleged was done on the *Teçora*: "Do your people routinely slaughter slaves?" he asks.

Covey answers, without waiting for Cinqué, that in Africa they are not really "slaves," for the Mende word is closer to "workers." This term may have been accepted by the film's consultant, Arthur Abraham, who in his *Mende Government and Politics* stressed the contrast between the forms of "unfreedom," or dependence, prevailing among the Mende (and the Yoruba and Ashanti) and the chattel or plantation slavery of the Americas. Most scholars, including those from Africa itself, while affirming that contrast, use the term *slavery* to describe an unfree status, which, however benign, was brought about by sale, seizure, or capture in war and involved coerced labor on the land or in a household. The Mende word for slaves is *nduwanga*.[21] Covey might better have answered the district attorney, "But our slavery is not like your slavery."[22]

The exchange between Covey and the district attorney points to an interesting possibility in the thought and sentiments of Cinqué and his fellow Africans—one not followed up in the film, but perhaps an explanation of the passion behind their revolt. In the film, the uprising and killing arise out of the horrors and cruel treatment on the voyages. These atrocities may have seemed all the worse because they were in contrast with the treatment of a *nduwe* back home. At best, slaves had a kin relation to their masters, especially slaves of the second or third generation; they were part of the household even while they suffered the stigma of slavery. At worst, they were uprooted and transported in shackles from one master to another, who might be harsh in denying them sufficient food or a proper place to live, but would not give them bloody beatings.

The uprooting and agony on the slave boats were startlingly worse. The wound may have become deeper as the Africans recollected the unpredictable paths by which they had come to the Middle Passage. Cinqué was seized and sold to a chief's son who, after a month, resold him to a Spaniard. As for his fellow prisoners, Yaboi was seized as a war captive, sold to a Mende man who kept him for ten years, then resold to a Spaniard. Bau was abducted on his way to plant his rice and taken directly to Lomboko and the boat. Pungwuni, of the Kono people, was sold by his mother's brother for a coat and, after two years' planting rice along with the wives and children of his African master, was sold by the latter to a Spaniard. Two of the girls on the *Amistad*, Maragru and Kagne, had been put up as pawns for their fathers' debts and sold when the men failed to pay. Young Teme, seized with her brother and widowed mother in the middle of night, was taken to the boat. "She never saw her mother or brother afterwards and was a long time in traveling to Lomboko."[23]

This rich detail was omitted from the film *Amistad*, an understandable choice given the constraints of time. Another omission from the film gives us more to ponder, for it was an immediate and frightening trigger to the revolt. Using sign language, Cinqué had asked the cook on the *Amistad* what was going to happen to the Africans; the cook had gestured that their throats would be slit and they would be chopped, salted, and eaten. Fear of white cannibalism went way back among the Africans. Young Olaudah Equiano wondered when he boarded his slaver whether "we were not to be eaten by those white men with horrible looks, red faces, and long hair." When his ship docked at Barbados, the Africans lay in the hold in "dread and trembling" lest they "be eaten by these ugly men." They stopped their cries only when some old slaves were brought on board to tell them they were not to be eaten, but made to work. For the historical Cinqué, as he recalled events later, the cook's prediction was the last straw, and it was then that he hid a nail to use for picking the lock on his chains.[24]

This episode is rooted in particular features of Atlantic life in the late eighteenth and nineteenth centuries. They help us understand the trauma of the Middle Passage and the panic that led shackled men to organize resistance. The omission from the film of so visually accessible and so brief a scene may be due not so much to time constraints as to a desire—already noted in *Spartacus*—to smooth away the idiosyncratic, the unmodern in one's heroes, anything that would make them too unpalatable "for contemporary audiences."[25]

In many ways, however, the film does recapture what was distinctive about the *Amistad* Africans. The Mende language, the mother tongue for most of them, is heard throughout the film, and spectators learn the meaning of the most important utterances from subtitles and from Covey. This verisimilitude is a long way from the American accents of the slaves from Thrace, Gaul, and Germany in *Spartacus*; the accented English of the rebels in *Burn!*; and the Spanish of the African and Afro-Cuban slaves in *The Last Supper*. If there are gains in portraying interaction through the convention of a common language in those films, there is another advantage in hearing Mende and English side by side and watching the struggle for communication.

The Mende insisting on their own funeral rites.

Amistad also shows other Mende customs being insisted on in the prison, to the mystification of the Americans. For instance, when one of the Mende dies, his countrymen will not yield up the body to the prison guards for burial, but hold it for their own ceremony. The filmmakers have served the Mende well in this scene, for among them any dead person not given a ceremony marking his or her "crossing the water" to join the ancestors will remain an earth-bound spirit, unhappy and perhaps troublesome to the living.[26]

If one were to reproach this admirable effort to reenact difference, it would be that it sometimes goes too far in the direction of "authenticity." The Mende learned English a little more fully than the film suggests: by January 1841 two of them wrote a letter in English to John Quincy Adams, and a few weeks later Cinqué himself wrote to his "Dear friend" Baldwin. In February 1841 *The Colored American* announced a mezzotint of the "noble Cinqué," with a facsimile of his handwriting, "although he came here a heathen, and unlearned."[27]

The Africans also assimilated Christian formulations more frequently than the film suggests. We see one of the Mende describing Christ's life to Cinqué through pictures in a Bible that had been handed him outside the courtroom, a fine example of Africans considering a Christian religious message on their own terms. But in fact they were barraged with Christian messages from the start: Louis Tappan had Yale divinity students trying to give them "God palavers" even before they could understand a word of English, and then continuing with an interpreter. At one of their services for the dead, the Africans permitted Rev. Leonard Bacon, a critic of slavery, to get in a prayer in English, even while the prisoner Shuma spoke over the corpse in the Mende language. In Cinqué's letter to Baldwin, he complained that their jail warden Pendleton, who had chained their hands, was a man who did "not think of God," a phrase he might have used to please Baldwin, but he might also have been able to assimilate to the Mende high god Leve, or Ngewa. *Amistad* rightly tells its story from the point of view and through the agency of the Africans rather than the Christian missionaries, but there was some overlap in agendas for a time.[28]

Cinqué is played with marvelous force, expressiveness, and conviction by Djimon Hounsou. As with Spartacus and José Dolores, the charisma of leadership is well suggested by the charisma of the performance. (Sebastián in *The Last Supper* is different, for he is a loner and an inspiration in his unstoppable rebellion, but becomes a leader only at the end of the supper and the morning of the revolt.) Back home in the Mende country, leadership was sanctioned for chiefs by their success in war or the success of their forebears—men with much land and many slaves. For senior figures in the Poro, the secret society that initiated all Mende youth, leadership came from their expertise in communicating with the spirits and their control of Mende traditions. Cinqué was clearly not in the first category, but perhaps he had brought over skills learned from the Poro. In his first dealings with Baldwin, he misrepresented the precise origin of his fellows, fearing that their villages might be harmed.[29]

In the changed circumstances of a Connecticut prison, the filmmakers decided to give aura to Cinqué's leadership through his role as a lion killer who had saved his family and his village. Another of the *Amistad* Africans was in fact a noted hunter who had killed five leopards and three elephants, and boasted of the leopard skin hanging in his hut in the Mende country. In the film, in contrast, Cinqué expresses doubt about his achievement and must be talked into speaking for the captives. Earlier, too, his face has an expression of horror when he kills the captain of the *Amistad*, though he never expresses remorse. In adding this complexity to the character of his Mende hero, Spielberg was following a path he had been compelled to open with the "deeply flawed" hero of *Schindler's List*: Nazi party member, egoist, money maker, rescuer of Jews, and finally a man regretful that he has not saved more. Cinqué is, of course, a much more sympathetic figure than Schindler, but giving the charismatic hero his moments of hesitation is an interesting speculation about a historical personality.[30]

In his comment to John Quincy Adams about his ancestors, Cinqué shows no trace of uncertainty before the camera. We come finally to that imagined exchange between Cinqué and

Adams, and Adams's fictitious reference to Cinqué in his speech before the Supreme Court. Cinqué's statement of how he will gain support from his ancestors for the trial ahead expresses a version of central Mende belief: "I've got my ancestors. I'm calling to them . . . to beg them to come to help me. I will reach back and draw them into me and they must come. For at this moment I am the whole reason they have existed at all." For the Mende, ancestral spirits act in the world, attentive to the well-being of their progeny. They are also intermediaries between their living descendants and Ngewa, a channel for the high god's benevolence. Rather than "draw in" the ancestors, as in Cinqué's phrase, a Mende would supplicate them: "O family members, help us; because long ago you [lived] among us, and you gave birth to us. Therefore we are coming before you, and do not remove [yourselves] from us."[31] Cinqué's affirmation in the film is close to this view.

Adams is superbly performed by Anthony Hopkins. In his early seventies in 1839–41, Adams was witty, learned, outspoken, possessed by "self-torment," as he said, and by a sharp temper he fought to control, politically ambitious, shrewd, and devoted to the public good of his country. At the time of the *Amistad* affair, Adams had changed from the patrician nationalist of his presidential years in the 1820s, when he had been concerned for roads, waterways, and cultural institutions that would bind together a nation run by gentlemen. Now he was an ardent fighter in Congress and in the new Whig party, and he successfully sought and won popular support for his causes. The gag rule of 1835, a southern initiative, was one of his major targets for nine years: it provided that any abolitionist petition to the House would automatically be tabled and not be available for consideration. He was not an abolitionist himself: he believed that the Constitution did not give Congress the power to legislate abolition within the states, and he also thought abolitionists too precipitate and

inflammatory in their program. Yet he was in frequent communication with abolitionists, and wrote in his diary at the end
of 1838:

> The conflict between the principle of liberty and the fact of
> slavery is coming gradually to an issue. Slavery has now the
> power, and falls into convulsions at the approach of freedom.
> That the fall of slavery is predetermined in the Counsels of
> Omnipotence I cannot doubt; it is part of the great moral
> improvement in the condition of man, attested by all the
> records of history. But the conflict will be terrible.

When the *Amistad* case came along, as Sean Wilentz has said,
"JQA had an opportunity to fight the Slave Power without com-
promising his nationalism or attacking the Constitution."[32]

The *Amistad* Africans had an effect on Adams, not through
actual conversations with Cinqué, but through other means. He
mastered a multitude of documents pertaining to their case, read
and heard about Cinqué and his fellows, became convinced of
the "abominable conspiracy, Executive and Judicial, of this Government against the lives of those wretched men," and asked
himself, "Oh, how shall I do justice to . . . these men?" After the
case was won, Adams was changed: he felt stronger in his deter-
mination to struggle against the slave trade no matter how fierce
the opposition. He was old, his faculties were failing, but three
weeks after the verdict he asked: "What can I do for the cause of
God and man, for the progress of human emancipation, for the
suppression of the African slave-trade? Yet my conscience presses
me on; let me but die upon the breach." He pushed for investigation of the complicity of the United States consul at Havana
with American, Spanish, and Portuguese slave traders; and he
helped distribute copies of his Supreme Court speech in hopes it
would aid the antislavery cause.[33]

That speech followed an excellent plea by Baldwin and lasted some eight hours over two afternoon sessions.[34] Cinqué was not present, being in prison in Westville with the other Africans. Adams did not call him a hero like Patrick Henry, whose name should be known to schoolchildren, but compared Cinqué and Grabeau to Harmodius and Aristogiton, Athenian conspirators against tyranny two thousand years before.[35]

Adams did, however, refer several times to the Declaration of Independence. Gesturing to a copy posted on a pillar, he said: "I know of no other law that reaches the case of my clients but the law of nature and of Nature's God, on which our fathers placed our national existence." Again, he insisted: "The moment you come to the Declaration of Independence that every man has a right to life and liberty, an inalienable right, this case is decided. I ask nothing more in behalf of these unfortunate men than this Declaration." Though Adams's legal argument hinged on the wrongful complicity of the president with the demands of the Spanish government, the interference of the executive with the courts, and the earlier *Antelope* case, he always led it back to the illegality of the slave trade and the freedom of the Africans. By what right did the secretary of state extend his sympathy to the two Cuban slaveholders, who had perpetrated "acts of lawless violence" against the Africans, and deny his sympathy to the very men "who had restored themselves to freedom?" "Has the 4th of July, '76, become a day of ignominy and reproach?"

Thus, the founding fathers of the American Constitution were evoked at the pleadings on behalf of the *Amistad* Africans, as they are also in the film. John Quincy Adams's words were pointed because his father, John Adams, had been among those founders. Adams ended by referring to other ancestors: the former justices of the Supreme Court, whom he had pled before as a young attorney, now all gone. He prayed that the present judges would likewise "act [their] part" so that the Lord would one day welcome them, "Well done, good and faithful servant." Adams wept as he ended, said the correspondent for *The Colored American*, as did he himself and other listeners.[36]

These words echo Cinqué's comment about ancestors to Adams in the film, and Adams's use of that comment in his plea. At its best, this cinematic fiction suggests an interesting cross-cultural parallel among the roles that ancestors, ancestral spirits, and ancestral precedents have in very different settings. Some anthropological practice today urges us toward such a thought experiment.[37] The realization of the thought experiment in the film is so literal and implausible, however—Cinqué tells Adams, who tells the Court in front of Cinqué—that it loses its provocative freshness, and many viewers shrug it off. There could have been other solutions: Cinqué might talk of the ancestors to encourage his fellow Africans; then later, during Adams's speech, the scene might cut once or twice between Adams and Cinqué as they each speak of their forebears. Here the camera would offer the parallel to the viewer (as Kubrick did with the speeches of Crassus and Spartacus in *Spartacus*), rather than assert it through an unlikely chain of communication.

For Cinqué, "crossing the water" had once meant the passage of the living to join the dead ancestors. The nightmare of the Middle Passage cut him off from the land of his progenitors and from his wife, son, and two daughters. When he recrossed in December 1841 on the *Gentleman*, he found his village destroyed. Spielberg could have ended *Amistad* simply with the triumphant image of the boat departing for Africa and the magnificent Cinqué in white looking at the sun in the east. But Spielberg does not want us to forget the pain of loss. In *Schindler's List*, one of the most searing scenes is that of the little girl, her coat red in the somber black and white of the picture, running alone in the street and hiding as the Jewish ghetto is emptied in Kraków by Nazi troops. The final legend of *Amistad* is equally somber: "His village was destroyed and his family gone. It is believed they were sold into slavery."

≡≡≡

Toni Morrison first learned of the woman she was to make the heroine of *Beloved* in the early 1970s in a published scrapbook of clippings and pictures about black life in America.[38] An article from the *American Baptist* told of "A Visit to the Slave Mother Who Killed Her Child" in February 1856 by P.S. Bassett of the Fairmount Theological Seminary in Cincinnati. A white antislavery preacher, Bassett gave a sermon in the prison and then went to the cell of the woman "concerning whom there has been so much excitement during the last two weeks." She was holding an infant with a swollen forehead. She explained to Rev. Bassett that when the slave hunters came to the house where she and her family were hiding after their flight, she hit two of her children on the head with a shovel, cut the throat of another, and tried to kill the one in her arms. She cared little what happened to herself, "but she was unwilling to have her children suffer as she had done." She had not acted in madness, she insisted, but "would much rather kill them at once . . . than have them taken back to slavery and be murdered by piece-meal."

The woman wept as she spoke of her own days and nights of suffering as a slave, and the preacher marveled at her satisfaction at freeing the child she had killed from such travail and the "passionate tenderness" of her maternal love. "She is about twenty-five years of age, and apparently possesses an average amount of kindness, with a vigorous intellect, and much energy of character."

In the cell with her was her mother-in-law, a woman in her sixties and a professing Christian, who told Bassett of her own life as a slave, of her eight children, most of them separated from her, and of her master, so "brutal and exacting" that in her old age she had decided to flee. "She witnessed the killing of the child, but said she neither encouraged nor discouraged her daughter-in-law—for under similar circumstances she would probably have done the same." The mother-in-law looked forward to the day when she would be delivered from her oppressor and would dwell with the Lord.

These were the fruits of slavery, Bassett noted—indeed, of slavery in nearby Kentucky, where it was supposed to be mild.

Toni Morrison was deeply struck by this story: "It was absolutely the right thing to do, but she had no right to do it." "The Slave Mother Who Killed Her Child" seemed to her to have resonance for contemporary uncertainties about the character of women's love—the slippage of nurturing love into obsessive, controlling love and the negotiation of the distance between love of someone else and love of oneself. It also had a bearing on contemporary feelings about abortion. As a story about the past, it seemed a perfect exemplar of the predicament of the African-American woman in slavery. "Motherhood was freedom for this slave woman," Morrison said. "She was trying to be a parent and a mother and have something to say about her children's lives in a slave system that said to blacks, 'You are not a parent, you are not a mother, you have nothing to do with your children.'"[39] Then events turned so that she destroyed what she had mothered and became haunted by her past.

During the 1970s, historians began to examine anew both the maintenance of black family life under slavery and the flight from slavery as forms of resistance that were more important and more frequent than revolts. It was not easy for slaves to do either. Persons of slave status had no formal right to marry, just as in Spartacus's day; their unions and parenting could be interfered with by sale and separation, and their intimate life might be troubled by the predatory sexual demands of slaveholders. Time for themselves was eaten up by labor for their owners ("I been so exhausted working," said a woman who had been a slave in Kentucky, "I was like an inch-worm crawling along the roof"); meanwhile, the master and the mistress thought the "family" the slaves belonged to was their plantation household. An earlier school of scholarship had seen these constraints and assaults as shipwrecking black family life; newer research on the history of women and of family has looked more carefully at what African Americans did about them.

Weddings were fashioned, often presided over, by a black religious virtuoso and included their own rituals, such as jumping over a broomstick. Sometimes these festivities took place behind the owners' backs; other times, as in All Saints Parish, South Carolina, the master and mistress stopped by the feast to drink a toast. Children were born, and parents gave them names that sustained a network of kinship; surnames were assumed that never found their way into plantation records. Couples living on different plantations saw each other when they could, the wives depending on women friends and kin for support in the interim. When a spouse was sold far away, a wife might say, as one did in a Richmond slave market, "my heart was a'most broke." If sold apart from her children, a mother might "bend to the ground," as one did in Kentucky, "weeping as if her heart was broken, asking the good Lord to let her die." And when a child was sold, as happened to fourteen-year-old Louisa Picquet, her mother's wailing prayers to the Lord to protect her followed her for the rest of her life.[40]

Running away was, as John Hope Franklin and Loren Schweninger said in a recent study, a major challenge to the slave system: "no matter how determined, compassionate, or brutal, [slave owners] remained unable to halt the stream of slaves that left their plantations and farms." Family loyalties were among the many considerations that played in the decision to flee and risk patrols, dogs, recapture, punishment, and harsher enslavement.

Husbands who had been sold separately from their wives ran away to rejoin them even when it meant living in hiding. Children and young teenagers who had been sold ran away to find their parents or other kin. Women were a much smaller percentage among fugitives than men, primarily because it was hard to escape with children, and the dangers of being on the run would press hard on the youngsters. Still, husband, wife, and children sometimes tried to get away together despite the difficulties of finding food and hideouts. Some women left on their own with their children, such as Pleasants and her four sons and daughters; she was finally recaptured and gave birth to a fifth child in a Virginia county jail. Once in a while mothers left their children behind, trusting that a grandmother or other women slaves would take care of them.[41]

And then there was the fugitive slave mother from Kentucky who fled to Cincinnati in 1856 with her four children and tried to kill them all when the slave catchers tracked them down. After Toni Morrison decided to tell her story, she sought a few details about the woman and her children: her name was Margaret Garner and she had two older boys, a daughter, and a baby girl. It was not easy in the 1980s to find more information outside of manuscripts and old newspapers. Morrison read extensively about slavery in general and about abolitionists, fugitives, and Cincinnati in the mid-nineteenth century. As for Margaret Garner, she said, "I really wanted to invent her life."[42]

Beloved is set in 1873 in Cincinnati, eighteen years after the arrest of the woman Morrison renamed Sethe. In the novel, Sethe is deep in trouble with the wounds of her past, her suffering while a slave, and her killing of her little daughter in order to save her. The "serious work" of her days is "beating back the past,"[43] but she can't stop her house from being haunted by her daughter's ghost. Her remaining daughter, Denver, lives haunted as well, not knowing the story but sensing its horror. Paul D arrives, once a slave at Sethe's plantation, torn by his own memories of humiliation and death and now seeking family. Into this house comes a strange young woman, Beloved, whom Denver and Sethe take to be the lost daughter returned. The book charts the shifting emotional economy of the household as Beloved gradually absorbs all of Sethe's love and attention, and Sethe and Paul D learn about each other's past. The book ends with the healing of Denver and the possibility of healing for Sethe. This surfacing from trauma comes in part from another strand of memory: the memory of the words and soothing hands of Baby Suggs, Sethe's mother-in-law, who had lived and died in the same house.

Morrison has written a novel about "the interior life of a small group of people," but its meanings flow out on all sides from that center. The injury done to Sethe on the plantation and her assault on her children call forth, through Morrison's wondrous plot and metaphors, a wider wave of violence. In the midst of answering questions from Beloved and Denver about her own mother, Sethe suddenly remembers what she had learned as a little girl from a kind woman, Nan, in the language her mother spoke. Nan and her mother had come across the ocean from Africa together and had both been raped by the crewmen. Sethe's mother had thrown away the baby that resulted when it was born, as she had other babies conceived from white men. Only Sethe's father had she put her arms around. Beloved's description of and reveries about the watery place from which she had come connect her with Sethe and womb, but they also call forth the horrors of the Middle Passage and those drowned on the way:

> I am always crouching. The man on my face is dead . . . I do not eat . . . if we had more to drink we could make tears. We cannot make sweat or morning water so the men without

skin bring us theirs . . . in the beginning we could vomit . . . now we cannot . . .

We are not crouching now . . . we are standing but my legs are like my dead man's eyes. I cannot fall because there is no room . . . the sun closes my eyes . . . those able to die are in a pile . . . the men without skin push them through with poles . . . they fall into the sea which is the color of bread.[44]

In Morrison's novel, Beloved is a ghost from Sethe's life, but also from the many crossings. The dedication page to *Beloved* reads "Sixty Million and more."

≡≡≡

Already in 1989 Oprah Winfrey was talking about producing a film of *Beloved* in which she would play the role of Sethe, and not long afterward her company, Harpo Productions, took out an option on Morrison's book. A celebrated television journalist, interviewer, and book discussant, Winfrey had a very different girlhood from that of her slightly older contemporary Debbie Allen, the initiator of *Amistad*. Allen's father was a dentist in Houston, and her mother, a distinguished poet. Winfrey's mother was young and unwed; her grandparents, who raised her in her early years, were farmers in Mississippi; and her father, with whose family she lived as a teenager in Nashville, had a barber shop and a grocery store. Her youth was marked by a wild interval, when she was sexually abused by a relative, but also by a noteworthy performance at high school and college. She developed a love of reading, with the writings of Harriet Tubman, Sojourner Truth, and Maya Angelou among her favorites in her early days. While Debbie Allen was marching with the civil rights protesters, Oprah Winfrey was eschewing African garb and what she considered the excessively militant politics of her classmates at Tennessee State.

Out of these experiences and her years of achievement on television, she has developed certain moral and political attitudes: empathy with the suffering of African Americans in slavery, and especially with women and children who have been harmed and abused, then and now; faith in the therapeutic value of bringing terrible things out in the open—as she did when she talked frankly on her TV show about being sexually abused; and belief that taking responsibility for one's own life is a better reaction to hardship than being paralyzed by "victimhood." She feels herself part of a black tradition—"I carry with me the voices of the women who have gone before me"—but also affirms that "the greatest contribution you can make to women's rights, to civil rights, is to be the absolute . . . best at what you do." This cluster of sentiments helps account for the attraction of her first cinematic role. It was in Steven Spielberg's 1985 film, *The Color Purple,* drawn from Alice Walker's novel: Winfrey played Sofia, a tough and self-respecting woman who walks out on her husband when he won't stop beating her.[45]

These same attitudes help explain her ardent desire to produce *Beloved* and take on herself the role of Sethe. After reading the novel, Winfrey began to collect slave memorabilia, including the records of various plantations, and to sense the lives of the men and women whom she met there. She was "involving herself in a process whereby," in the words of bell hooks's summons to black women, "we see our history as counter memory, using it as a way to know the present and invent the future." In making the film, Winfrey explained, "I wanted people to be able to feel deeply on a very personal level what it meant to be a slave, what slavery did to people, and also to be liberated by that knowledge." To her scriptwriter and her fellow producer, she said, "This is my *Schindler's List.*"[46]

Morrison had never thought of *Beloved* becoming a film. Her art and vision are, she says, in the play and richness of language, and she feared that a cinematic rendering would be reductive.

But an artist should not consider her work "inviolate," so she agreed to Winfrey's project. The writing of the script she left to others, though she offered advice at many different stages of the filmmaking. Winfrey discussed possible directors with her and finally settled on Jonathan Demme. Morrison knew and respected his *Silence of the Lambs* (1991) and *Philadelphia* (1993); she had heard, too, of his great collection of Haitian art and his concern for the people of Haiti. She felt he was a "man of principle and taste" who would take black life seriously, but not be "reverential" about it. It seemed the right mix for directing *Beloved*.[47]

Beloved was Demme's first genuine historical film, but some of its concerns figure in his earlier work. He had made two documentaries about black people in different worlds—*Haiti: Dreams of Democracy* (1987) and *Cousin Bobby* (1991) about Harlem—and several of his films depict women trying to take charge of their lives. *Beloved* also has a plot and themes that lend themselves to Demme's own aspirations over the years. As Michael Bliss and Christina Banks have said in their recent study, Demme has explored the troublesome and violent features of American culture in his films, but they are seasoned with a comic sense of human weakness. His films end with an added sense of possibility, if only in the feelings people have about themselves or in their sentiment of closeness to others.[48] Some of the visual motifs from his earlier films also surface again in *Beloved*, here reversed and with new meanings.

Set in the nineteenth century, *Beloved* clearly cannot replay the late twentieth century. Danny Glover, who starred in *The Color Purple*, among many other films, was cast as Paul D; Beah Richards, another old trouper, played the grandmother, Baby Suggs; and two young actors, Kimberly Elise and Thandie Newton, took the roles, respectively, of Denver and Beloved. Demme wondered whether they should be given special lessons in dialect and accent, perhaps to reproduce in the film the pronunciation and language found in the 1937–38 Federal Writers' Project interviews with former slaves. Morrison discouraged this idea: the characters speak, as they do in her book, with slight accents and in a rhythmic dialect usually close to standard English.[49] Bernice Johnson Reagon, a folklorist and performer, was sought as a consultant to the remarkable composer Rachel Portman. Research was done on what Cincinnati looked like and how people dressed in the decades after the Civil War. But the historical power of the film comes even more from the interactions of the characters and the traces of the past on their bodies and their minds.

≡≡≡

The film opens with a gravestone marked "Beloved" at the back of a snowy cemetery. The camera gives us a long shot of a wooden house, 124 Bluestone Road, on the outskirts of Cincinnati in 1865. The camera enters the noisy house to show a scene of disruption, with floors shaking and household articles and the dog flying through the air. The two teenaged sons take their things and leave home in the turmoil, while their mother, Sethe, remains calm, tending to the dog. Their sister, Denver, bereft at her brothers' departure, goes for comfort to her old grandmother, Baby Suggs.

We move ahead eight years to the summer of 1873. The film will now follow the events in 124 Bluestone through the seasons of one year. Until mid-winter the activities in the house are interspersed with flashbacks, as people tell each other of things that happened during the time of slavery and also recall the preaching of Baby Suggs.

The action begins with the arrival of Paul D on the dusty road in front of the house. A former slave at Sweet Home with Sethe and her husband, Halle, he tells her he has been walking for years. She tells him that Baby Suggs, her mother-in-law, has died. They enter the house through a flashing crimson light. Paul D realizes that the house is haunted, and Sethe explains without anguish that the haunt is not Baby Suggs, but her baby daughter. Her sons have run off, but she has her daughter, Denver, with her, the child she was carrying when she fled Sweet Home. Denver comes down the stairs, a lovely but sullen eighteen-year-old, resentful of Paul D's presence and weeping about their isolated life: "No one speaks to us, no one comes by. Nobody even knows I'm alive."

Paul D suggests to Sethe that they should move from the haunted house, but Sethe answers no. "I've got a tree on my back and a haunt in my house and nothing in between but the daughter in my arms. No running . . . I'll never run from another thing." A violent haunting of the house occurs, with a table just missing Paul D. Sethe then recounts to Paul D the events of their planned flight eighteen years before, the most terrible of them shown in very short flashbacks as she speaks. She herself was pregnant, even though still nursing a baby girl. Halle had not met her, so she had sent the three children ahead with the cart. The plot discovered, one of the slaves was hanged; Paul D, she recalled, was put in a neck iron; and the sons of Schoolteacher, the master, had seized her and sucked the milk from her breasts. The Schoolmaster ordered one of his sons to whip her on the back, and she had fled without finding Halle.

Paul D opens the back of Sethe's dress to find the tree of scars left by the beating and kisses her back. They make love in a hasty way. Paul D has a nightmare where we see, with him, the horrors of that same night.

A subsequent exchange between Paul D and Sethe takes place as she tends the corn in her garden. Sethe defends her life, claiming she has kept Denver "from the other one," the life she would have had under slavery: "I won't let the past back in my yard." Paul D warns her of loving anything that much and wonders if there would be room for him in her life. They agree to see how it goes. That night Denver tells her mother that she senses that the baby ghost has left the house and that she misses her.

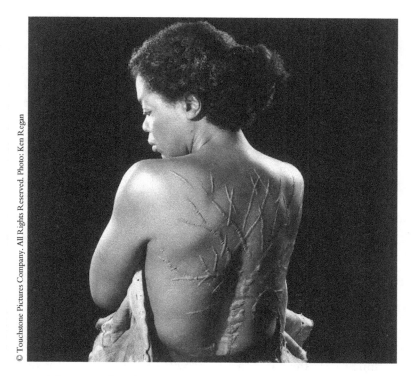

© Touchstone Pictures Company. All Rights Reserved. Photo: Ken Regan

The next day the camera follows the emergence of a young woman from the bluish mist of a stream near the house. Well-dressed but wet, she drags herself to a stump in front of Sethe's house and lies on it, ignoring the insects crawling all over her. Meanwhile, Paul D, Sethe, and Denver have gone to a carnival on the blacks-only day, an unusual venture for Denver, who rarely leaves the yard. They enjoy themselves, and Paul D wins a smile from Denver. Returning, they find the young woman, who tells them in a strange voice that her name is Beloved.

The camera follows the shifting relations in the enlarged household over the next few months. Denver warms to Beloved, who she suspects from the beginning is her sister returned, as she helps her to walk and dances with her while Sethe is away cooking in a restaurant in Cincinnati. Denver has moments of jealousy, when Beloved seems to know something of "diamonds"—crystal earrings—in her mother's past that she, Denver, has never heard of. Both young women listen attentively when Beloved asks Sethe to talk of her own mother: "Your woman never fix up your hair?" "Momma don't talk about her," Denver interrupts. But Sethe does begin to talk, explaining that her mother had to start work so early in the morning that she hardly knew her. Pressed by Beloved to go on, Sethe has a sudden return of memory. She sees her mother and others on the plantation being gagged and hanged. A woman talks to little Sethe in an African tongue, "That is your mother. Your mother and I were taken by many men, many times. Only you she gave a name. She put her arms around only your father." Spectators of the film see this scene with Sethe in flashback, but to Denver and Beloved she says only that her mother was hanged, she doesn't know why.

Denver and Beloved also exchange confidences. After their dance in the attic, Denver asks Beloved what it was like before she came to them. Beloved tells her it was small and hot, with nothing to breathe down there, and with lots of people, some of them dead. She, Beloved, was in the water, the diamonds were there, and then "she left me behind." Beloved asks Denver to recount how she had been born in a little boat. In flashback we see the flight of the bruised and bleeding pregnant Sethe from Sweet Home. A young white woman named Amy Denver, eccentric and slightly mad, comes upon Sethe and helps her give birth to her baby in a tiny boat. Sethe's face is filled with tears of joy and triumph as she realizes she has reached the Ohio River. Stamp Paid and his fellow black boatmen take Sethe and her baby across to Baby Suggs on the free side. Sethe explains that Halle hasn't made it yet, greets her sons, and nurses her newborn and her older daughter, to whom she shows her crystal earrings. Baby Suggs puts her hands on Sethe's head and says to her, "God has led you home. Lay down your sword and shield," and the flash-back ends.

As the summer moves into autumn, Paul D and Sethe become closer in body and soul, even while their relationship is troubled by Beloved's efforts to come between them and by more discoveries about the past. Their scenes of love are tender and ardent, with the camera showing that both of them have trees on their backs from their beatings. But they squabble about Beloved, of whom Paul D is suspicious: "I see why she is holding on to you, I just can't see why you're holding on to her." When Sethe remarks bitterly that Halle seems to have abandoned her, Paul D tells her for the first time what happened that night at Sweet Home. Halle saw Schoolteacher's sons take her milk, went mad, and died. The next day Sethe goes with both Beloved and Denver to a clearing in the woods, where they can think about Denver's daddy. Sethe tells the girls about Baby Suggs's preaching at that spot, and the grandmother is shown in a wondrous flashback. "Let the children come. Let your mothers hear you laugh." And the children laugh. "Let the grown men come. Let your wives and children see you dance." And the men stamp and dance.

When the women return to the house, Paul D is in his bath and he embraces Sethe. Beloved sees them, runs away in fright, and, over the next few days, directs erotic glances at Paul D. Very bothered, Paul D keeps reaching for Sethe, but one night he drags himself out to the barn. Beloved follows him, insists that he "touch her on the inside part," falls on him, and, in agony, he has intercourse with her, as the room around him glows red.

Deeply ashamed at what has happened, Paul D rehearses telling Sethe the next afternoon after work, but instead says he wants her to become pregnant. They walk back to the house in delighted laughter as the first snowflakes of winter fall. The next day at his job at the Cincinnati pig pens, Paul D tells his good news about starting a family to Stamp Paid. Stamp Paid shows

Paul D an old clipping from the newspaper and tells him that Sethe had killed her daughter.

Paul D returns to confront Sethe, who begins her account, "Only thing I ever did on my own, using my own head." She describes the glorious twenty-eight days of her freedom after her arrival. We then see in flashback another of Baby Suggs's sermons in the woods: "Love your flesh, love it hard. Yonder they do not love our flesh." On the twenty-ninth day the slave catchers come with Schoolteacher and one of his sons. Sethe rounds up her children in the little barn and, when the men enter, her sons are on the ground, one daughter has her throat cut, and Sethe is swinging her newborn in the air. Baby Suggs revives the boys, while Schoolteacher spits out "animal."

After hearing this account, Paul D reproaches Sethe: "What you did was wrong, Sethe . . . There must have been some other way." Sethe defends herself: "I stopped 'em. I put my babies where they'd be safe." Paul D thinks this is misdirected love; he says cruelly that Sethe has two feet, not four, and leaves.

For the rest of the winter months through spring, 124 Bluestone is a house of the three women. Sethe decides soon after Paul D's departure that Beloved, who knows Sethe's lullaby and has a scar on her throat, must be her murdered baby who has come back to her. She will never let her go away again and spends all her savings in gifts, garments, food, and dried flowers. The three rejoice for a while, but Sethe is fired from her restaurant the first time she is late, and gradually the money and food run out. Beloved greedily demands all of Sethe's attention, and threatens violence to Sethe and herself. In despair at her mother's state and at Beloved's behavior, Denver has a vision of Baby Suggs, who tells her she must go out by herself sometime, she must go out into the busy world of black people and white people whom she can see crossing back and forth on the dusty road in front of 124 Bluestone.

Denver goes out alone to the black neighborhood and tells her former schoolteacher that her mother is ill. Food begins to arrive at their doorstep, sent by the black women who have snubbed the family in the past but won't leave them in distress. Denver ventures into Cincinnati to see the Bodwins, the abolitionist sister and brother who had saved Sethe from being hanged back in 1856 and had given Baby Suggs the house on Bluestone Road. She pours out the story of Beloved and Sethe to the housekeeper there, who had known and admired her grandmother. The housekeeper promises that Denver can work evenings for the Bodwins, and immediately takes the story of the ghost to the black ladies of the community. They decide that though a mother should not kill her children, children can't just up and kill their momma.

The camera returns to Bluestone Road on a hot summer's day, where Sethe is chopping ice to keep Beloved cool and does not hear Denver say she is going off to work. As Denver waits on the porch for Mr. Bodwin, the black ladies of the community come to the their house and begin their prayers and cries of exorcism. Sethe comes out on the porch with a naked and pregnant Beloved. The exorcisers gasp, but continue. Mr. Bodwin drives up in his horse and cart, and Sethe imagines it is the Schoolteacher once again. She runs at him with the icepick, but is stopped by Denver and the women. At the same moment, Beloved disappears, and all that is left on the porch is Baby Suggs's quilt, which she had been holding.

The scene switches to the streets of Cincinnati some weeks later, where a neat and shaven Paul D sees Denver looking very sure of herself and grown up. She has a job, is studying with Miss Bodwin, and has a beau. She tells him that Sethe has not got out of bed since the day Beloved disappeared and adds, "You don't have to stay away, but you watch how you talk to my momma." Delighted with Denver's new life, Paul D visits Sethe and tells her that Denver will take care of her in the day and he in the evenings. When Sethe weeps, "She leave me . . . Paul, she my best thing," he answers, "You're your best thing." "Me? Me?" Sethe asks wonderingly.

The film ends with a flashback of Baby Suggs preaching in the woods on the theme "Love your heart, more than the womb . . . more than the private parts . . . Love your heart. This is the prize, amen." As she says hallelujah, shakes hands, and kisses the children, the camera gives a last long shot of 124 Bluestone Road, now peaceful.

≡ ≡ ≡

In the movement from the miraculous prose of Toni Morrison to the screen, the story of *Beloved* has lost some of its breadth, complexity, and imaginative range. But its central messages—historical and human—have been sustained and, in some ways, enhanced by the gifts of the innovative Jonathan Demme and his associates and by the talent and commitment of the actors. We see in the film the wounds of slavery, inflicted and then self-inflicted through resistance—or, rather, we see the *memories* of these wounds as they still disturb the free. We see the resources of an African-American community for defining these wounds, for quarreling about them, and for healing them. The story of trauma and recovery is distinctive, but it is told so as to invite others in, into the haunted house at 124 Bluestone and into Baby Suggs's clearing in the woods.

The costs of slavery to black women are measured in the film especially in regard to mothering. On many plantations in the South, slave women were encouraged to breed children to replenish the labor supply, but it was not always with men they chose, and once the child was born they were often denied time to take care of it.[50] This is an old story for Sethe, we learn as she combs out Denver's hair: she speaks of how her mother had to get in line so early she never had time for her. The sudden return of the image of her mother's hanging amid burning flames and of the forgotten words of her mother's friend Nan make Sethe stiffen with surprise: she jumps up and crosses the room to fold sheets and hide her dismay. Her mother's friend spoke not only of sexual abuse—being "had by many men, many times"—but of wanting to be a mother on one's own terms: "Little Sethe, only you she gave a name, she put her arms around only your father." The abuse that rankles in Sethe's own past is that the Schoolteacher's sons took her milk, the milk for her baby. "They took my milk, they took my milk," she repeats to Paul D as we see for an instant this dreadful scene.

A slave lullaby from the American South tells of the sorrow of the mother who must care for the mistress's baby (perhaps even wetnurse it), not her own:

> Hushaby, don't you cry,
> Go to sleepy, little baby.
> When you wake, you shall have cake.
> And all the pretty little horses . . .
> Way down yonder in the meadow,
> There's a poor little lambie;
> The bees and the butterflies pickin'
> out his eyes,
> The poor little thing cries, "Mammy."[51]

Lullabies are sung overvoice in *Beloved*, and Sethe has composed one of her own, though none of them has precisely the words and melody of "Hushaby." But the bees and the butterflies are there, sometimes in close up, through the camera of Jonathan Demme and his director of photography, Tak Fujimoto. They are in the fields around Sethe early in the film, and again in the cornfield, before she and Paul D talk. Butterflies surround Beloved as she first emerges from the water. Later, at the height of her demands on Sethe, when she threatens to strike her mother, then scratches at her own throat and wails like an infant, the camera moves to bees buzzing on the window pane. The insects here are not terrifying like the butterflies of the serial killer James Gumb in *Silence of the Lambs*. They are uncanny and unsettling in their beauty, however, and evoke Sethe's predicament.

Sethe denies on the surface that there is a predicament in regard to her mothering as a free woman: the ghost baby is "sad," but Sethe can live with it. She assures Paul D that she has kept her children from "that other life" where their eyes would be picked out. Paul D reminds her that her sons have run away from the haunted house and that her eighteen-year-old daughter won't go beyond the yard. When he finds out how her other daughter died, he says, "There must be another way."

Infanticide was a little-practiced form of resistance among slave women in the American South, and surely little discussed. There are only two mentions of it in the hundreds of narratives of ex-slaves collected by the Federal Writers' Project. Elizabeth Fox-Genovese tells of a slave mother, living probably in the 1850s, who could no longer bear to see her children sold by the master when they were a year or two. With her fourth child, so the story went, "she got up and give it something out of a bottle and purty soon it was dead. 'Course didn't nobody tell on her or he'd of beat her nearly to death." "Smothering" their infants was an accusation made by slaveholders against slave mothers on occasion, but recent American scholarship is divided on how often these were accidental deaths and how often intentional. Linda Bryant, the slightly fictionalized heroine of Harriet Jacobs's autobiography, describes her mixed feelings when her infant son became very ill during her days as a slave:

I loved to watch his infant slumbers, but always there was a dark cloud over my enjoyment. I could never forget that he was a slave. Sometimes I wished that he might die in infancy. God tried me. My darling became very ill . . . I had prayed for his death, but never so earnestly as I now prayed for his life; and my prayer was heard. Alas, what mockery it is for a slave mother to try to pray back her dying child to life! Death is better than slavery.[52]

Whatever the general case, when Margaret Garner's murder came before the court in Cincinnati in January 1856, it attracted much public interest, opponents calling it a "deed of horror," an inhuman act, and abolitionists giving support. Lucy Stone, for example, reported on her visit to the "poor fugitive" in prison: "I . . . took her toil-hardened hand, and read in her face deep suffering and an ardent longing for freedom . . . I told her that a thousand hearts were aching for her, and they were glad that one child of hers was safe with the angels." Garner's act was also defended by a male writer for the *Provincial Freeman,* a black abolitionist paper: "May her spirit be fostered wherever the land is polluted with the unhallowed feet of those accursed beings, namely Slaveholders! 'Give me liberty or give me death,' were the words of Patrick Henry." Of course, it would have been even better to cut the throats of the "lawless pursuers."[53]

The film *Beloved* incorporates this range of attitudes within the black community and within Sethe's breast. She has saved her daughter, she insists to Paul D, and her cutting her throat was not the act of an animal. Yet Sethe's own dread of her deeds that day is shown in the flashback of her agonized and defiant expression as the slavehunters open the barn door—a difficult moment very well acted by Lisa Gay Hamilton, who plays the younger Sethe.

© Touchstone Pictures Company. All Rights Reserved. Photo: Ken Regan

There is yet another element in the trauma of the past, this one drawing more fully on the painful recollections of Paul D. Slavery has left its mark on their flesh. Sethe talks of this scar in her reminiscence about her mother: one day, when she was little, her mother had shown her the brand on her body and told her that it was the mark by which she could know her if anything happened to her face. Sethe had answered, "Mark me too," and her mother had slapped her. The camera shows the other marks: the tree of scars on Sethe's back and then, as the two become lovers, the tree on Paul D's back as well. The scars gleam as the embracing bodies turn.

Once again we have an interesting development in Demme's cinematic work with the human body. In his early days under Roger Corman, the major rule was to "keep the action going and the flesh showing."[54] In *The Silence of the Lambs*, the fate of the woman's body is at the fore, as Clarice and other FBI agents (and the film's viewers) see photos of and hear about skinned corpses, and as the serial killer James Gumb sews a woman's skin into a garment for himself. In the film, flesh is frightening, and the spectator is frozen beyond pity. In *Philadelphia*, Andy's skin becomes ravaged with the lesions of AIDS; in the film, we are called to compassion as life drains away from him. In *Beloved*, the scarred flesh can be wept about, kissed, and loved in tenderness and passion.

Sethe has told Paul D that she "won't let the past in her yard," but, of course, the past is fully in her house as the baby ghost. The belief in haunting was widespread among African Americans in the nineteenth century, and among other Americans as well. Ghosts are not only a part of the folktale tradition, but were also remembered by the elderly ex-slaves telling their stories to the Federal Writers' Project. "Of course dar is haunted houses," said 103-year-old Mary Woolridge, who had been a slave in Washington County, Kentucky. Ninety-nine-year-old Sophia Ward of Clay County, Kentucky, reported that her own master had not been as mean as most, but that the slave owner nearby "wuz so mean to his slaves that I know of two gals that killt themselfs," one of them after he had whipped her almost to death for forgetting to put onions in his stew. Their ghosts came and stood over his bed at night until he left his house, moved to Richmond, and committed suicide himself. Gertrude Vogler of Wayne County, Kentucky, who had all her nine children in the years after emancipation, recalled that the ghost of her son Charlie had come back from the graveyard. But he had not visited her, only her son Ed. "If [Ed] was livin' right, he would not be seeing Charlie every night."⁵⁵

Talking about ghosts in conversation or a novel is a different matter from depicting them in a film. A haunted house, according to the witness of former slaves in Kentucky, has doors banging, objects moving noisily, and animals propelled across the room. When today's audiences see such goings-on in the film *Beloved*, after so many poltergeist movies, they seem hackneyed and even funny.

But Demme and Fujimoto have also used color and light to suggest haunting and haunts, and this technique works. Red is the most important and the most sinister, a color associated with wickedness in ghost lore. Paul D first enters 124 Bluestone Road through a frightening red glow; for an instant an image of Sethe holding her slain daughter pulsates at the back of the house. Later, a red glow lights up the little barn when Beloved and Paul D are having sexual intercourse, and, as he weeps, it turns into the red of the dawn. Early in Beloved's stay, a ghostly white light streams through the window onto the young woman as she offers to make bread with Sethe; Sethe can hardly see that she is there. And the attic in which Denver and Beloved exchange confidences is suffused with blue light.[56]

Beloved is a complex figure in the film: the ambiguity and multiple associations in Morrison's novel are somewhat reduced, while an interesting possibility is opened. Most notably, explicit reference to the trauma of the Middle Passage is gone: little Sethe is not told (as in the quotation above from the novel) that her mother crossed the ocean from Africa and was raped by crewmen on the boat, but only that her mother had been had by many men. Beloved's reverie (quoted above from the novel—"I am always crouching . . .") is not heard, but only her words to Denver about being hot down there and in the water. The association of this underworld with those drowned in the crossing can still be made by viewers—the bluish light in the attic as Beloved speaks reminds us of water—but the association with the waters of birth and rebirth is stronger. Denver goes on to describe her own birth in a little boat (a good boat, not a slaver) filled with Sethe's birth waters and the free waters from the Ohio River. Earlier, when Sethe first sees Beloved, who had just arisen from the stream, she runs and makes water in the field.

Beloved is primarily a baby who has returned at a grown-up age, and less a figure for the drowned on the Middle Passage. Either coincidentally or intentionally, the young woman cast as Beloved, Thandie Newton, has light skin. Her appearance raises an interesting question for the viewer, one noted in the novel and in the historical evidence as well. In the novel (though not in the film), little Sethe is told that her mother had babies by white men who raped her, on the boat and afterward, but that she "threw them away." In historical reports (though not in the novel), the little girl slain by Margaret Garner was described as "almost white" and the father may have been Garner's master.[57] Beloved in the film may suggest another trauma of slavery, the baby conceived through a forcible union.

In Newton's agile performance, Beloved plays both the baby and the young woman. She is angry, as a ghost must be who feels she has been wronged in life and abandoned by her mother, and now wants to make up her loss by total possession of the loved object. She also wants to dispossess her mother in Paul D's arms and become the one with a new baby in her belly. But Beloved does not stand only for the repressed sorrows of the past; she is a catalyst in bringing them to the surface. Linda Krumholz, in an insightful essay on Morrison's novel, has related Beloved to the Trickster figure in the African-American folk tradition.[58] This is true of the film as well, where the viewers are never quite sure who Beloved is, and Paul D and finally Denver herself have their doubts. Each member of the family is turned around for better or for worse by Beloved.

Beloved's energy is not just destructive, however. Through sweetness, she induces both Sethe and Denver to tell things about the past, some never said or remembered before. Talking is a step toward healing, as we see also in the exchanges between Sethe and Paul D.

The major healer is Baby Suggs, her name reprising the theme of birth and rebirth. Somewhat simplified from the novel, where she has a sourer sense of the "nastiness of life," Baby Suggs is still a mighty figure in the film, played with charisma by Beah Richards. We see in her an interesting and original variant on the religions practiced among African Americans in the last decades of slavery and the early years of freedom. For the ills of the body and for social grievances, slaves could turn to the medicines and spells of conjurers, who were for the most part men. Yet many an ex-slave remembered the healing skills of his or her mother: "My ol' mammy were great fo herb doctorin'," Celia Henderson said of her girlhood in Kentucky and Tennessee, "an I holds by dat too a good deal." The spirits of the dead could be called up for advice by specialists in the rituals of voodoo or hoodoo, and these figures included women. Female prophetesses were reported on some plantations, such as Maum Katie from the Sea Islands in Georgia, "an old African woman, who remembers worshipping her own gods in Africa . . . [with] tremendous influence over her spiritual children." Black preachers, with their own expressive blend of Christianity and African religion, had their gatherings in slave churches or in the woods ("Dey wuz an ol' man he were powerful in prayer an gather de darkies unda a big tree," Celia Henderson remembered). In these places, praying, singing, and stamping inspired spirit possession and conversion. Though the

© Touchstone Pictures Company. All Rights Reserved. Photo: Ken Regan

preachers are ordinarily described as men, there must have been some women with the calling of Sojourner Truth, who, soon after she became free in New York state, was a "miraculous" preacher in a perfectionist community.[59]

Baby Suggs's domestic healing is through hands, not herbs: she pats and strokes Sethe's sons back to life; she holds Sethe's head to give her strength and calmness; and she clasps Denver's body to give her courage to go out in the world. Her preaching in the woodland clearing has the same cadence as a black sermon urging the message of Jesus or repentance, but her call is to the resurrection of the flesh—here in this world—from the injuries and contempt of slavery. The ex-slave Hagar Brown remembered that when the clapping, stamping, and singing expanded the spirit within her slave church in South Carolina, "heart commence to turn over!"[60] Baby Suggs starts from the heart, which she enjoins her listeners to love, as she does their flesh. Her preaching in the woods, which are suffused with green and yellow, completes the poignant affection with which Sethe and Paul D can accept each other's scarred bodies.

Baby Suggs is dead when Beloved arrives, and she can give advice to Sethe and Denver only in memory and in vision. The final exorcism is accomplished by the community of black ladies of Cincinnati, who use Christian and non-Christian objects, prayers, and wails against the ghost. When Beloved disappears, a host of beautiful butterflies swarms around Baby Suggs's quilt, lying on the empty porch of 124 Bluestone, but this time they summon us to think not of danger but of metamorphosis and resurrection.

≡ ≡ ≡

As with *Amistad*, the major actors in *Beloved* were deeply affected by their roles, which drew remarkable performances from all of them. "Each had an epiphany in the film," Toni Morrison commented. Oprah Winfrey wept the day the tree of scars went on her back. Daniel Glover was deeply moved by his final words to Sethe, "You your own best thing." Beah Richards, herself from Mississippi, said the role of Baby Suggs was "what I was born for."[61]

But the tale of Margaret Garner continues to unfold. Initially inspired by the reading of Morrison's novel, Steven Weisenburger researched all the sources on Garner's life and the legends about her, and published his fascinating *Modern Medea* in 1998, about the same time as the film was premiered. The story and its traumas have a somewhat different shape, though Garner resembles Sethe in her absolute commitment to the need for freedom—a quality as important as the air one breathes. The escape party from Kentucky was large that night in January 1856: Margaret, her four children, her husband, Robert Garner (who lived on a nearby plantation and saw Margaret once a week), and Robert's parents. Their freedom in Cincinnati lasted only a day, for their hideout was discovered. In the subsequent trial, which won national attention and the active participation of abolitionists, Archibald Gaines's claim to the return of his slaves under the Fugitive Slave Act was honored. Weisenburger shows that it became clear—though never stated openly in court—that at least the slain daughter and maybe two other of Margaret Garner's children had a white father and that he was probably Gaines, who was seen "carrying little Mary's body and sobbing uncontrollably over her corpse."[62]

Returned to slavery, the Garner clan was sent by Gaines down the Mississippi to a family cotton plantation. On the way, their steamboat had an accident, and in the turmoil Margaret Garner and her ten-month old daughter Priscilla were either thrown from the boat or Margaret herself jumped with her daughter in her arms. Priscilla drowned; Margaret was saved. The family lived together doing hard labor, but at least without interference in their intimate life from the master. Two years later, in 1858, Margaret Garner died of yellow fever, and her last request to her husband, as he recalled, was "never to marry again in slavery, but to live in hope of freedom, which she believed would come in some way."[63] He followed her wishes, running away to serve in the Union army during the Civil War and marrying again only later.

Toni Morrison's Sethe, Oprah Winfrey's Sethe, and Steven Weisenburger's Margaret Garner all stand in different relations to the evidence, but each in her way gives us historical insight. Each woman haunts us with the tragedies and hopes of the past.

5

Telling the Truth

WHEN FILM CRITICS and moviemakers classify films, they often use genre terms: westerns, gangster movies, film noir, police stories, romantic comedies, and the like. History movies, when not classified as "epics," are called "period films" or "costume dramas," terms that grate on historians' nerves. It would be possible to cram the films we have been considering into these categories. *Spartacus*, *Burn!*, and *Amistad* could be thought of as "epics," though they stretch the genre with their complexity (especially the last two) and their mixed endings.[1] *Burn!* might also be named a "war film." From some points of view *Beloved* is a "horror movie," and one could quite reasonably say, in thinking of the development of Denver, that it is a "coming of age" film.

Let us change the grid for a moment and ask, What kind of historical inquiry do these films make? From *Spartacus* to *Beloved* we see quite a range. *Spartacus* is primarily a film about politics—about political struggles among Romans and a major political/social revolt against Roman power. It depicts the social distance between free and slave, rich and poor. It also introduces interesting erotic and tender elements into the story through both the sexual excitement that masters find in slaves and the desire for progeny among the slaves.

Burn! and *The Last Supper* are infused with the concepts of political economy and the theories of historical materialism, but with different time frames and emphases. Pontecorvo treats his subject on a grand scale over a number of years, while Gutiérrez Alea settles his story elegantly within the five days of Holy Week. *Burn!* portrays economic interest in terms of political control, foreign investment, trade, and labor, whereas *The Last Supper* does so in terms of technological advance, production, and labor.

But these are feature films with absorbing personal stories, not analytical tracts. *Burn!* leads us through the changing characters of and relations between Sir William Walker and José Dolores. *The Last Supper* explores the interior conflicts of the count and the varied loyalties of the slaves, which finally converge around Sebastián. Both these films replace the ahistorical Spartacus, Varinia, and their companions, who could just as well be speaking at American political meetings of the late 1950s as in the Mediterranean and Germanic world of 73–71 BCE, with persons, customs, tales, and songs that have some pointed specificity, African or Afro-Caribbean. With the carnival and dances of *Burn!* and the Christian ceremony and Yoruba gods of *The Last Supper*, cultural history is merged with political economy.

Amistad and *Beloved* concentrate their stories within a few years, but expand their time perspective through flashbacks—and, for *Amistad*, flash-forwards. *Amistad*, like *Spartacus* and *Burn!*, is centered around political struggles, national and international, a revolt against wrongfully held power, and the claims of property. Its attention to political and legal thought, though flawed in realization, is stronger than in *Spartacus* and matches that of *Burn!*. In *Burn!*, Walker makes ironic reductionist arguments against slavery (as a prostitute is cheaper than a wife, so a paid worker is cheaper than a slave), while President Sanchez makes only a brief affirmation of liberty. *Amistad* draws more fully on the rhetoric of antebellum America.

Amistad also has a cultural nuance. The love of freedom is assumed by Baldwin and Adams to burn automatically in every human breast, but the film suggests a linkage of that desire in Cinqué and his fellows to certain features of Mende life and tradition and to the horrendous Middle Passage. The scenes on the slaver add a psycho-cultural approach to the past, depicting the degrading wound of that experience as lived, repressed, and remembered.

The film *Beloved* is a cultural and psycho-social exploration par excellence of the traumas of slavery and the struggle to resist it. Finally, the women's experience comes into its own. The story suggested in the vignettes of Varinia showing her son to Spartacus; of mothers holding their little sons up to José Dolores and of boys screaming in burned villages; of Cinqué's wife, doubly lost to him, walking with their son—that story is fully told in *Beloved* in a tragic version. Perhaps we could better say "tragicomic," since the film ends with a couple restored and a daughter coming into her own. Tragicomic, but not timeless. The shape of family life, the patterns of cruelty, the forms of resistance, the haunting pangs of guilt, and the processes of curing in *Beloved* all grow out of the relations of slavery at Sweet Home plantation and the cultural practices of the African Americans.

In the course of this book, I have noted that some of the shifts in cinematic treatment of slave resistance over the decades were parallel to or followed on similar changes in the work of historians. In some instances, the cinematic treatment was independent and even in advance of that by historians. For example, filmmakers, whose medium is visual and performative, were ready to see how carnival and religious ritual—the washing of the slaves' feet and the supper for the slaves—were not just coincidental to revolt but became preludes or avenues to it. They were drawn to the filming of ceremony, and this fascination helped them take ceremony seriously.[2]

Along the way, I have also asked about balance in these films, whether they make an effort to understand and depict the pressures on and motivations of the different parties involved. The filmmakers were not initially attracted to their projects by mere curiosity. History mattered to them because they identified with some injustice, or felt passion for human suffering, or sensed the horror of war and violence, or saw a hidden story of their own people that must be made known. There is nothing wrong with this motivation. Professional historians may also have such impulses or other critical intentions when they choose a project, but they are supposed to find ways to achieve balance and detachment before they are done.

The films have unequal success on this count, but none is so one-sided as to be dismissed as mere apologia. None of them depicts a kind slave master or mistress: only in *Beloved* is there a brief flashback of a good mistress, who gave Sethe the crystal earrings when she married and listened with indignation to her report of her milk being taken. None of the films investigates slaves contented with their lot: in *The Last Supper* the count's personal slave, dressed in livery, appears devoted to his master and eager to separate himself from the others; in *Spartacus*, Marcellus, the cruel trainer in Batiatus's gladiator school, is an ex-slave loyal to his employer. Yet because all these films are about resistance to slavery, rather than slavery in general, this scanty treatment is defensible.

All the films show a range in attitude among slave owners, ruling groups, or white people, as the case may be. Even in *The Last Supper*, much is extracted from the small world of the single plantation by the economical development of characters: the count, the mulatto technician Duclé, and the priest, each with his own inner conflicts.

As for the slaves and working people more generally, *Sparta-cus* goes farthest in the direction of treating them as heroic broth-ers and sisters: the infighting between Spartacus and Crixus, referred to in the sparse historical sources on the revolt, is muted in the film; Spartacus's troops are presented as fighting only when attacked first by the Romans and are never shown provoking battle or simply pillaging estates. In *Burn!* and *Amistad* there is unity among the Queimada rebels and the *Amistad* Africans, but black people are pictured as diverse, from the black soldiers, themselves ex-slaves, fighting against Dolores's men, if only for the money, to the Africans who seize their fellows for the slave trade. In *The Last Supper* the execution of the count's orders against the rebellious slaves is carried out by hired mestizos, without a drop of pity.

Relations among blacks are shown most richly in *Beloved*. In the film the white people range from the atrocious Schoolteacher and his vicious sons to the "good whitefolks," the Bodwins, who are abolitionists. Mr. Bodwin makes a momentary appearance, but the others are shown only in memory, and then, except for Amy Denver, very briefly. Even more than Toni Morrison's novel, the film concentrates on black people; and like the novel (and all of Toni Morrison's writing), the film portrays black people as human beings with their fears and loves, anger, guilt, jealousy, and affection. After playing his role as Paul D, Danny Glover explained why he saw the film as a breakthrough: "*Beloved* . . . is a story about how people make the adjustment into being full-fledged human beings, how they take their own freedom, entitlement to themselves as human beings, their own dysfunc-tionalism, neurosis, not seen in relation to white people."[3] Out of this intensely explored universe comes the convincing power of *Beloved*.

———————◆———————

In a book published at the time that *Amistad* premiered, Debbie Allen, Steven Spielberg, and others from DreamWorks talked about the making of the film and, more generally, about history and its uses. Meredith Maran and Anne McGrath remarked on uncertainties in knowledge of the past:

> The *Amistad* events actually happened. The images were there; the narrative occurred. Yet we cannot see the scene as it really was. Our eyes and our hearts are different. Even among people who were there, no single view holds "the truth." To see is to know—but only in glimpses, small fragments of an incomplete and always changing picture.

Spielberg echoed this sense of final unknowability in his comment about Cinqué: "No matter how earnest the artist's effort, he or she can never really capture, 'pin down,' or fully re-create the lives of great men and women." *Amistad*, the DreamWorks book concludes, is "a movie that blends fiction with true events."[4]

These quotations invite us to a final look at "fictionalizing" through the lens of the historian's rules about evidence. In *Spartacus*, "true events" were not a major concern, and some exciting historical possibilities were lost through indifference to evidence. *The Last Supper*, a film with narrow focus and a close collaboration between the filmmaker and the historian, had only two departures from the record (postdating the events a few years and letting one of the rebels survive), neither of them out of keeping with possibilities in late eighteenth-century Cuba. *Amistad* will be our case for examination, because we have been told so much about its making and because its quality as a historical film is in some ways so very good and in others disappointing.

Are the fictional elements in *Amistad* used to fill in the inevitable gaps in the historical record? Are they historically plausible, so they can effectively serve as "approximate truths" and "thought experiments"? Or do they override perfectly good historical evidence in a way that risks misleading?

As for the "look" of the past, Rick Carter, the production designer, found locations that would be appropriate settings for the action: El Morro, Puerto Rico, for the African and Cuban events; and Newport, Rhode Island, for New Haven street scenes, the court, and the exterior of the prison. Considerable artistry, ingenuity, and money went into giving "an overall impression of what it really would be like to be transported back into that time."[5]

Still, the historical significance of a film will hinge on the people and what happens to them. From this point of view, the most telling sets in the film are Cinqué's village, the holds in the *Teçora* and the *Amistad*, and the prison yard in New Haven. Filling in the gaps around Cinqué and the Africans is, on the whole, convincing and effective, as we have seen; and the composite characters of the black abolitionist, Joadson, and the English naval officer, Captain Fitzgerald, are plausible, though Joadson is a blander figure than the enterprising and militant James Pennington.

In contrast, there are inventions in the film that do not fill in gaps in the evidence or bring undervalued people and processes to the fore, but supplant clear evidence with an erroneous picture of antebellum politics and sensibility. The filmmakers invented the Catholic Judge Coglin for the second trial, a man whose religious conscience as an outsider leads him to a verdict in favor of the Africans. They invented an untried young property lawyer, "Roger Baldwin," who grows into a more principled person through his defense of and later egalitarian relation with Cinqué. The real Roger Baldwin, in contrast, was a middle-aged, experienced, and fighting abolitionist from the start. And they invented the ending of the speech by John Quincy Adams, in which he gives a sentimental and romantic version of his attitude toward Cinqué. None of these inventions can be justified in terms of a needed simplification of the story: indeed, the first two make the story more complicated. None of them can be justified in terms of required drama, for there is dramatic potential in the actual lives of Judge Judson and Roger Baldwin, and in the oratory of John Quincy Adams, which research and imagination could have teased out.

All three fabrications come from a wish to make patterns of alliance and friendship in New England in 1839–40 resemble egalitarian hopes in late twentieth-century America.[6] Wish fulfillment is a fine goal for certain genres of films (as for certain genres of writing), but it should not steer the imagination in a historical film. Adams expressed his empathy for the Africans in his *Memoirs* by the words "unfortunate" and "wretched." In his speech to the Supreme Court he genuinely applauded the actions of Cinqué and his fellows to free themselves, but in comparing their heroism with the "Lilliputian trickery" of the American rulers of a great Christian nation, he said, "Contrast it [the Lilliputian trickery of the U.S. secretary of state] with that act of self emancipation by which the savage, heathen barbarians Cinque and Grabeau liberated themselves and their fellow suffering countrymen from Spanish slave traders . . . Cinque and Grabeau are uncouth and barbarous names. Call them Harmodius and Aristogiton. . . ."[7]

Adams is caustic about "civilized" morality here, but the kind of appreciation he offers of the Africans is not consonant with Spielberg's idea of "my friend Cinqué, who was over at my place the other night," to quote Adams's Supreme Court speech in the film. Nor is that friendship ideal consonant even with the attitudes of Martin Delany, the son of a slave father in Virginia and a free black mother. Journalist, abolitionist, healer, and writer, Delany visited Liberia about fifteen years after Cinqué had returned to Sierra Leone. Delany wrote not about establishing friendship with the Africans he met, but about giving them garments, furniture, and missionaries.[8]

As it happened, sources were available to the filmmakers to create scenes of amity and feeling between these Africans and Americans. I cite two here, not to suggest that Spielberg was obliged to use them as such, but to insist that they should have provided the pattern for imagining relationship in the film, rather than transferring a model from our own time. One of the *Amistad* Africans, either Kale or the young lad Kali, sent a letter to Adams in the late winter of 1841, which was printed in the *Emancipator*. The letter speaks of friendship and makes claims for likeness between the Mende and Americans:

Dear Friend Mr. Adams:

I want to write a letter to you because you love Mendi [sic] people, and you talk to the grand court . . . We want you to ask the Court what we have done wrong. What for Americans keep us in prison? Some people say Mendi people crazy; Mendi people dolt because we no talk American language. Merica people no talk Mendi language; Merica people dolt? . . .

Dear friend Mr. Adams, you have friends, you love them, you feel sorry if Mendi people come and carry them all to Africa. We feel bad for our friends and our friends all feel bad for us . . . If American people give us free we glad, if they no give us free we sorry—we sorry for Mendi people little, we sorry for American people great deal, because God punish liars . . .

Dear friend, we want you to know how we feel. Mendi people *think, think, think*. Nobody know what we think; teacher he know, we tell him some. Mendi people have got souls. We think we know God punish us if we tell lie. We never tell lie; we speak truth . . . All we want is make us free.[9]

The other source is a description of the final goodbyes in a New York church between the Africans and the abolitionists who had been their support, including two African-American lay readers. Simon Jocelyn of the *Amistad* committee told once again of the tribulations of the Africans and how their story would help end the bondage of Africans in the United States. Margru, one of the three African girls, read Psalm 130; the Mende sang a song in their own tongue "with an energy of manner, a wildness of music and at times a sweetness of melody, which were altogether peculiar," and then concluded with an abolitionist hymn. The listeners wept.[10]

Neither source evokes a picture of Roger Baldwin and Cinqué exchanging hand and arm clasps in warm man-to-man bonding, as in their final goodbye in the film *Amistad*. Yet the pictures these sources call forth are at least as dramatic: tension and opacity on both sides, Americans sentimental and patronizing, Africans assertive and expressive, both reaching out across a considerable divide.

Why should a film with serious, even passionate, intention behind it, with much of value in it, both historically and ethically, with a stellar list of historical consultants and a $40 million budget go off track in this way? It is due, I think, to two habits of thought that we simply must shake. The first is too cavalier an attitude toward the evidence about lives and attitudes in the past. This evidence is all we have to go on, and it is where we begin in dramatizing a story. We must respect that evidence, accepting it as a given, and let the imagination work from there. If, after such an effort, we still decide to depart from the evidence—say, in creating a composite character or changing a time frame—then it should be in the spirit of the evidence and plausible, not misleading. Exceptionally, a historical film might move significantly away from the evidence out of playfulness or an experiment with counter-factuality, but then the audience should be let in on the game and not be given the false impression of "a true story."[11]

The second is a bad habit of underestimating film audiences. To be moved, entertained, instructed, and engaged by a historical film, spectators do not need to have the past remade to seem exactly like the present. According to a recent book on Steven Spielberg, he used "considerable dramatic license" in *Amistad* in order to make it "symbolic of a struggle that continues to this day" in the form of immigrants brought in illegally to work in sweatshops.[12] But the "dramatic license" in *Amistad* does not call to the viewer's mind the appalling exploitation of immigrant labor in the present day. Spectators are more likely to think of possible parallels between the past and the present if the strangeness in history is sustained along with the familiar. The Middle Passage and twentieth-century Holocaust reflect on each other effectively through the film because the scenes on the *Teçora* and the *Amistad* are left in their own time.

———◆———

By the end of the twentieth century, no producer is likely to brag, as Darryl Zanuck did in 1936, that he had made Rothschild an English baron and nobody even noticed. When Oliver Stone presented grainy black-and-white scenes in *JFK* so that they seemed actual footage from 1963, there was a public outcry. Much still remains to be done in finding ways to indicate the truth status of a historical film, not just in books and reviews afterward, but in the movie itself. Can there be lively cinematic equivalents to what prose histories try to accomplish in prefaces, bibliographies, and notes and through their modifying and qualifying words "perhaps," "maybe," and "we are uncertain about"?

To start with, makers of historical films should be willing to tell audiences, if only briefly, what they have done to shape a story. The old options—opening with "this is a true story" and/or ending with "any resemblance to persons living or dead"—are no longer acceptable.[13] Increasingly, though not in the films we have looked at in this book, filmmakers place a legend along with the final credits where they state they have followed an actual story, but have changed certain names or events in such and such a way. Filmmakers can surely invent fresh images and sequences to let their viewers in on the secrets of what they have done with the past.

Where does a historical account come from? Some of our filmmakers announce an immediate source in the credits: Howard Fast's novel in *Spartacus*, Toni Morrison's novel in *Beloved*, and William Owens's *Black Mutiny* in *Amistad*; the name of Manuel Moreno Fraginals, if not his *Sugarmill*, in *The Last Supper*. Other than that, these films provide viewers with only a few clues as to how their story has come down to us. None are explicit in *Spartacus*, *Burn!*, or *The Last Supper*, though, for *Burn!* (a composite tale) viewers would expect a story initially set down in confidential governmental reports. In *Amistad*, news of the seizure of the Africans is seen on the front page of two newspapers, each with different headlines—*The New Haven Register* and the *Emancipator*—and a listener in court is shown sketching the prisoners. It is also evident, as we watch, that an abundance of judicial and government documents were produced by the case. In *Beloved*, Paul D learns first of Sethe's slaying of her daughter through a crumpled newspaper clipping, and the help given to Sethe by the abolitionist Bodwin suggests that here, too, there would be abolitionist memoirs.

Other possibilities exist or could be developed. James Ivory's *Jefferson in Paris* has opening credits over Thomas Jefferson's writing machine, but then moves to 1873 in Ohio, where a reporter from the *Pike County Republican* is ferreting out a story from Madison Hemings, the son of Thomas Jefferson by his sister-in-law, the slave Sally Hemings. Madison Hemings says that the

Jefferson side of the family never discusses the Hemings, so we learn of an oral tradition and a silence before we go back to what happened in the 1780s.

Might one have had in *Spartacus*, at least for a moment, Plutarch musing over the pages he wrote on "Spartacus's war"? or the red-shirted republican liberator Garibaldi savoring a novel about Spartacus's feats, as he did in 1874? Might *The Last Supper* have opened not with the legend "The events shown in this film took place in a Havana sugar mill during Holy Week at the end of the eighteenth century," but with a member of the Royal Council reading the account of the uprising? Could the ex-slave Daniel Godard have appeared for a moment in *Amistad*, telling (as he did to the Federal Writers' Project interviewer) how he had heard as a boy about the "slave revolt, where that African prince, one of a large number of slaves that were kidnaped, took over the Spanish ship *L'Amistad*, killing two of the officers"?[14] His words evoke an actual living tradition, unlike John Quincy Adams's fictional nonstarter about schoolchildren and Patrick Henry.

Historical writers are supposed to let their readers know when their evidence is uncertain or when different views of the same episode exist. History is not a closed venture, fixed and still, but open to new discovery. In searching for cinematic equivalents to prose expression on these matters, we can be helped by the distinction made by theorists between "classical" film narrative and "art-cinema" narrative. Here we might consider pairs such as objectivity versus subjectivity, omniscience versus nonomniscience, and transparency versus reflexivity.

On the one side there is classical film narrative (traditionally used for many history films), in which spectators are invited to believe that they are looking right in at events and, through the camera's movement, are all-knowing about them. Here spectators are also encouraged to find a satisfactory explanation from the coherent and seamless unfolding of events. The classical film is "realistic," with shots often at eye level in the middle distance. On the other side there is a more subjective or "art-cinema" narration, in which spectators are not omniscient, but may be invited to see the action for a considerable time from the point of view of one character or simply denied information by the camera. Here spectators may also be distanced from the events, either because episodes do not flow smoothly into each other or because they are interrupted by a comment from outside, including reference to the representational status of the film itself. In the art-cinema narration, high and low angles, sudden shifts in lighting or sound, and other "unrealistic" effects can be frequent.[15]

These are useful but arbitrary distinctions, for classical narrative films can make good, if limited, use of the subjective and/or distancing effects. The five history films considered in this book are all of this composite type. Do they remind viewers at any point of the moments of uncertainty in the historical record? Do they distance the viewer from immersion in the events of resistance to slavery in a way that widens perspectives? Although these are not the central concern in any of the films, there are some such elements nonetheless. *Spartacus* and *Amistad* have the most consistently classical narratives, though the astonishing longshot of the Roman legions in Spartacus's last battle and the intense close-up of Cinqué's face and bloody fingers as he works out the spike can remind viewers that they are both in and outside the action. We spectators are cast as omniscient through all of *Spartacus* and *Amistad*, and through much of *The Last Supper* and *Beloved*—we see events now from Sethe's or Paul D's or Denver's or Beloved's point of view—yet we are on the whole privy to them all.

Burn! is more experimental: much of the time we see what is going on in Queimada through Sir William Walker's eyes or through his telescope. The widow of the executed rebel Santiago is opaque to him, and does not reveal anything to us either, though we can make a guess about what she and her villagers think through the funeral ritual. Once José Dolores has emerged as a leader, we see him for a time outside Walker's vision—joyous, troubled, determined—but after Walker's return to the island ten years later, Dolores is hidden from Walker and from us until his capture. Only at the very end of the film do we learn directly what Dolores thinks, when we hear him speak, out of Walker's hearing, to the soldiers about the future, and finally to Walker himself: "But what civilization? Till when?"

Burn! also has moments of metacommentary. Walker's stylized and choruslike observations about history—its sudden transformations and ironies—encourage spectators to think beyond the action on Queimada. Perhaps Sir William Walker, who tries to make history follow his rules and is undone when its carnivalesque and recalcitrant elements get beyond his control, serves also as a figure for the unpredictable elements (like Brando himself) in making a film about the past. Characters in some of the other films, too, might recall to us the powers of storytellers to make things happen: the haunt Beloved, who is finally undone, and the Yoruba Sebastián, who blows magic powder on his master's face and survives.

There are also unsettled questions in all five films which can leave viewers with a sense that history is open, not congealed. *Spartacus*, *Burn!*, *The Last Supper*, and *Amistad* have in them slaves who serve their masters (there are almost no mistresses in these films) in silence. A doorman at the presidential palace offers his blessings to José Dolores, but mostly these people go about their business. What are they thinking? *Beloved*, with its light-skinned ghost, leaves unresolved the question of whether memories conceal as well as reveal, a question that is put more sharply in Morrison's novel and in Weisenburger's *Modern Medea*. And, finally, viewers may well ponder what happens to the eloquent and energetic Cinqué when he returned to Africa. Some said he became a Mende chief, a slave-trader, and a polygamist in Sierra Leone before returning in his last days to the Christian mission.[16]

Films can do much more to pose questions to their viewers about history-making and history-knowing. Readers may recall Kurosawa's *Rashomon* of 1950, where four different persons implicated in a rape give four different accounts of what happened; or Karel Reisz's *French Lieutenant's Woman*, where a Victorian love affair is pictured in parallel with an affair between the actors playing these roles in film. Danny Glover, the actor who played Paul D in *Beloved*, has been trying to find a producer for a film about Toussaint L'Overture and the revolution on Saint-Domingue.[17] Perhaps that story could be told in parallel with the fascinating life of the premier historian of that revolution, the cricket player, writer, and social critic C.L.R. James.

Historical films should let the past be the past. The play of imagination in picturing resistance to slavery can follow the rules of evidence when possible, and the spirit of the evidence when details are lacking. Wishing away the harsh and strange spots in the past, softening or remodeling them like the familiar present, will only make it harder for us to conceive good wishes for the future.

But putting aside historical films as wish fulfillment does not mean putting aside historical films as a source for hope. I end with a figure of hope, a perfect example of how film can bring to life a person on the boundaries of historical possibility: Baby Suggs, stretching out her arms in the green and golden woods of free Ohio, calling children to laugh, preaching of the redeemed heart at the human core, bringing the magic of her old hands, her voice, and smile to the young who encircle her. "Hallelujah!" she cries as she touches them and kisses them. "Hallelujah!"

Notes

Chapter 1: Film as Historical Narrative

1 François Hartog, *The Mirror of Herodotus: The Representation of the Other in the Writing of History*, trans. Janet Lloyd (Berkeley: University of California Press, 1988), chaps. 7–8; S.C. Humphreys, "From Riddle to Rigour: Satisfactions of Scientific Prose in Ancient Greece," in Suzanne Marchand and Elizabeth Lunbeck, eds., *Proof and Persuasion: Essays on Authority, Objectivity, and Evidence* (Brussels: Brepols, 1996), 3–24; Thucydides, *The Peloponnesian War*, trans. R. Crawley (New York: Modern Library, 1934), 1.1.10, 1.1.19–22.

2 Aristotle, *The Poetics*, in *On Poetry and Style*, trans. G.M.A. Grube (Indianapolis: Bobbs-Merrill, 1958), chap. 9, 1451b; chap. 23, 1459a.

3 Thucydides, *Peloponnesian War*, 1.2.22. The classic studies of historical narrative are Hayden White, *Metahistory: The Historical Imagination in Nineteenth-Century Europe* (Baltimore: Johns Hopkins University Press, 1973), and Hayden White, *The Content of the Form: Narrative Discourse and Historical Representation* (Baltimore: Johns Hopkins University Press, 1987).

4 Walter Rodney, *West Africa and the Atlantic Slave Trade* (Nairobi: East African Publishing House, 1969); *A History of the Guyanese Working People, 1881–1905* (Baltimore: Johns Hopkins University Press, 1981); Derek Walcott, *Omeros* (New York: Farrar Straus Giroux, 1990), 3.28.1.

5 An insightful book showing the inventive craft and mixture of genres found in "nonfiction film" is Charles Warren, ed., *Beyond*

Document: Essays on Nonfiction Film (Hanover, NH: University Press of New England, 1996). Among professional historians, Robert Rosenstone has been one of those arguing most forcefully that historical feature films should be evaluated seriously as "real history": Robert Rosenstone, "The Historical Film as Real History," *Filmhistoria* 5 (1995): 5–23; Robert Rosenstone, ed., *Revisioning History: Film and the Construction of a New Past* (Princeton, NJ: Princeton University Press, 1995), 3–13, 202–13; and Robert Rosenstone, *Visions of the Past: The Challenge of Film to Our Idea of History* (Cambridge: Harvard University Press, 1995). Other studies in the burgeoning commentary by historians on film include Marc Ferro, *Cinema and History*, trans. Naomi Greene (Detroit: Wayne State University Press, 1988); Pierre Sorlin, *The Film in History: Restaging the Past* (Totowa, NJ: Barnes and Noble, 1980); Peter C. Rollins, ed., *Hollywood as Historian: American Film in a Cultural Context* (Lexington: University Press of Kentucky, 1983); Mark C. Carnes et al., eds., *Past Imperfect: History According to the Movies* (New York: Henry Holt, 1995); Robert Brent Toplin, *History by Hollywood: The Use and Abuse of the American Past* (Urbana and Chicago: University of Illinois Press, 1996): Toplin's book considers the production of the film as well as its content. Useful forums evaluating film as a way to recount the past have appeared in the *American Historical Review* 95 (1988): 1173–1227, with essays by Robert Rosenstone, David Herlihy, Hayden White, John E. O'Connor, and Robert Toplin; and in *Perspectives* 37, 4 (1999), "Reel History: A Special Issue," edited by Robert Toplin and followed by an important exchange between Robert Rosenstone and Robert Toplin in *Perspectives* 37, 8 (1999): 19, 23–25. Among journals devoted to the subject is *Film and History*, founded by John O'Connor and now in its twenty-ninth year, and *Vertigo. Esthétique et histoire du Cinéma.*

6 Edward P. Thompson, *The Making of the English Working Class* (London: Gollancz, 1963); Emmanuel Le Roy Ladurie, *Les Paysans de Languedoc*, 2 vols. (Paris: S.E.V.P.E.N, 1966); Eugene Genovese, *Roll, Jordan, Roll: The World the Slaves Made* (New York: Vintage Books, 1974).

7 Vladimir Nizhny, *Lessons with Eisenstein*, trans. and ed. Ivor Montagu and Jay Leyda (New York: De Capo, 1979), 24.

8 David Bordwell, *Narration in the Fiction Film* (Madison: University of Wisconsin Press, 1985), 3–26. I am indebted to Bordwell's study and to that of George M. Wilson (*Narration in Light: Studies in Cinematic Point of View* [Baltimore: Johns Hopkins University Press, 1986]) for their lucid and well-documented examination of how films communicate.

9 Interview of Gillo Pontecorvo with Julio Medem, <www.ofcs.org/article10.html>.

10 Dan Georgakas and Lenny Rubenstein, eds., *The Cineaste Interviews: On the Art and Politics of the Cinema* (Chicago: Lake View Press, 1983), 311: interview with Gillo Pontecorvo.

11 These issues are given excellent review by Joyce Appleby, Lynn Hunt, and Margaret Jacob, *Telling the Truth about History* (New York and London: W.W. Norton, 1994).

12 See Anthony Grafton, *The Footnote: A Curious History* (Cambridge, Mass.: Harvard University Press, 1997).

13 Eileen Power, *Medieval People* (1924; London: Methuen, 1966), chap. 2.

14 See, for instance, George F. Custen, *Bio/Pics: How Hollywood Constructed Public History* (New Brunswick, NJ: Rutgers University Press, 1992), 111–18: "The Research Departments and Their Bibles," and Edward Maeder, ed., *Hollywood and History: Costume Design in Film* (Los Angeles: Los Angeles County Museum of Art; New York: Thames and Hudson, 1987), 10–16.

15 Marina Warner, *Joan of Arc: The Image of Female Heroism* (London: Weidenfeld and Nicolson, 1981), 140–58, quotation on 142.

16 Rosenstone, ed., *Revisioning History*, 7.

17 Carl Theodor Dreyer, *Dreyer in Double Reflection: Translation of Carl Th. Dreyer's Writings "About the Film" ("Om Filmen")*, trans. Donald Skoller (New York: Dutton, 1973).

18 Custen, *Bio/Pics*, 37–38, 138–39. Zanuck is not quite right when he adds, "there never was a Rothschild a Baron": George III never gave Mayer Amschel Rothschild or his sons this title in England, but in 1822 his five sons were made barons in Austria. See Vivian Mann and Richard I. Cohen, *From Court Jews to the Rothschilds: Art, Patronage and Power, 1600–1800* (Munich and New York: Prestel and the Jewish Museum, New York, 1996), 94.

Georgakas and Rubenstein, eds., *Cineaste Interviews*, 129 (interview with Francesco Rosi); see also the comment of Bernardo Bertolucci about his film *1900*: "I tried to respect history as much as possible" (145).

19 Eric Foner and John Sayles, "Eric Foner and John Sayles," in Carnes et al., eds., *Past Imperfect*, 17.

20 Bordwell, *Narration*, chap. 3; Wilson, *Narration*, chap. 1.

Chapter 2: Resistance and Survival: Spartacus

1 Derek Elley, *The Epic Film: Myth and History* (London: Routledge and Kegan Paul, 1984), 198; Robert Sklar, *Film: An International History of the Medium* (New York: Harry N. Abrams, 1993), 61; W.E.B. Du Bois, *The Suppression of the African Slave Trade to the United States of America* (New York, 1896); Everett Carter, "Cultural History Written with Lightning: The Significance of *The Birth of a Nation*," in Peter C. Rollins, ed., *Hollywood as Historian: American Film in a Cultural Context* (Lexington: University Press of Kentucky, 1983), 9–19; Leon F. Litwack, "*The Birth of a Nation*," in Mark C. Carnes et al., *Past Imperfect: History According to the Movies* (New York: Henry Holt, 1995), 136–41. On Wilson's attitudes, see especially Woodrow Wilson, *Division and Reunion, 1829–1889* (London: Longman, 1893).

2 Gary A. Smith, *Epic Films* (Jefferson, NC, and London: McFarland, 1991), nos. 181, 182, 190.

3 C.L.R. James, *Black Jacobins: Toussaint L'Ouverture and the San Domingo Revolution* (New York: Dial Press, 1938); Herbert Aptheker, *American Negro Slave Revolts* (New York: Columbia University Press, 1943), 368–74.

4 M.I. Finley, ed., *Slavery in Classical Antiquity: Views and Controversies* (Cambridge: Cambridge University Press, 1960); M.I. Finley, *Ancient Slavery and Modern Ideology* (London: Chatto and Windus, 1980); David Brion Davis, *The Problem of Slavery in Western Culture* (Ithaca: Cornell University Press, 1966); Laura Foner and Eugene Genovese, eds., *Slavery in the New World* (Englewood Cliffs, NJ:

Prentice Hall, 1969); Eugene Genovese, *Roll, Jordan, Roll: The World the Slaves Made* (New York: Vintage Books, 1974).

5 For an example of film criticism subordinating any aesthetic or historical components in films to present-day purposes and messages, see Maria Wyke, *Projecting the Past: Ancient Rome, Cinema and History* (New York and London: Routledge, 1997). Kubrick's *Spartacus* becomes a vehicle for everything from communist labor ideas to propaganda for Zionism and the Cold War (60–72).

6 Stanley M. Elkins, *Slavery: A Problem in American Institutional and Intellectual Life* (Chicago: University of Chicago Press, 1959), chap. 3; Eugene Genovese, "Rebelliousness and Docility in the Negro Slave: A Critique of the Elkins Thesis," *Civil War History* 13 (December 1967): 293–314.

7 Kirk Douglas, *The Ragman's Son: An Autobiography* (New York: Pocket Books, 1988), 276–77.

8 Howard Fast, *Being Red* (Boston: Houghton Mifflin, 1990), 269, 276–77, 286.

9 Douglas, *Ragman's Son*, 280–84; Dalton Trumbo, *Additional Dialogue: Letters of Dalton Trumbo, 1942–1962*, ed. Helen Manfull (New York: M. Evans, 1970), 483–84, 531; Bruce Cook, *Dalton Trumbo* (New York: Charles Scribner, 1972), 270–71; Dalton Trumbo, *Night of the Aurochs*, ed. Robert Kirsch (New York: Viking, 1979), ix–x, xiii.

10 Trumbo, *Night of the Aurochs*, ix–x; Trumbo, *Letters*, 484, 521–22 (Dalton Trumbo to Peter Ustinov, [1959]); Douglas, *Ragman's Son*, 297, 333; Cook, *Trumbo*, 272, 309, 311–12. In his critique of Kubrick's rough footage of *Spartacus*, Trumbo insisted on complete reshooting of the scenes that followed the climatic battle. These scenes concerned in particular the actions of Batiatus, Gracchus, and Crassus.

11 Peter Ustinov, *Dear Me* (London: Heinemann, 1977), 217–19; Simon Callow, *Charles Laughton: A Difficult Actor* (London: Methuen, 1987), 247; Trumbo, *Letters*, 484, 521–22. Trumbo called the script "remarkably unstable," but was a good sport about considering changes in the lines.

12 Douglas, *Ragman's Son*, 258, 287–88. Though Douglas talked specifically about hiring Jay Sebring to make authentic hair-dos

for the slaves, Alicia Annas has described Douglas's cut as Spartacus as "distinctly non-Roman," and Varinia's hairstyle as fitting
with the late 1950s. Edward Maeder et al., *Hollywood and History:
Costume Design in Film* (New York: Thames and Hudson, for the
Los Angeles County Museum of Art, 1987), 63, 197.

13 Joseph Gelis, *The Film Director as Superstar* (Garden City, NY:
Doubleday, 1970), 314 (interviews with Stanley Kubrick,
1968–69).

14 Gelis, *Film Director*, 295–99; John Baxter, *Stanley Kubrick: A Biography* (New York: Carroll and Graf, 1997), 238, 264, 278, 298.

15 Baxter, *Kubrick*, 140, 147.

16 An excellent study is Lily Ross Taylor, *Party Politics in the Age of
Caesar* (Berkeley and Los Angeles: University of California Press,
1949).

17 T. Robert Broughton, *The Magistrates of the Roman Republic*, 3
vols. (New York: American Philological Association, 1951–86),
1: 493, 524; 2: 1009–132; Taylor, *Party Politics*, chap. 1; W. V. Harris, "*Spartacus*," in Carnes et al., ed., *Past Imperfect*, 43.

18 Callow, *Laughton*, 248–50.

19 Recent studies of Roman slavery with full bibliographies are
Keith R. Bradley, *Slaves and Masters in the Roman Empire: A Study
in Social Control* (New York and Oxford: Oxford University Press,
1987), and Keith R. Bradley, *Slavery and Society in Rome* (Cambridge: Cambridge University Press, 1994).

20 Plutarch, *Crassus*, and Appian, *Roman Civil Wars*, 1, 14, as given
by Thomas Wiedemann, *Greek and Roman Slavery* (London:
Croom Helm, 1981), 216, 220. Studies of Spartacus's revolt can be
found in Keith R. Bradley, *Slavery and Rebellion in the Roman
World, 140 B.C.–70 B.C.* (Bloomington and Indianapolis: Indiana
University Press, 1989), chap. 5; Catherine Salles, *Spartacus et la ré-
volte des gladiateurs* (Brussells: Éditions Complexe, 1990); and Brent
D. Shaw, *Spartacus and the Slave Wars: A Brief History with Documents* (Boston: Bedford Books, forthcoming).

21 Tony Curtis and Barry Paris, *Tony Curtis: The Autobiography* (New
York: William Morrow, 1993), 186; Douglas, *Ragman's Son*,
292–94; Bradley, *Slavery and Society*, 28.

22 Information on the origins of gladiatorial fighting and gladiators can be found in Ludwig Friedländer, *Roman Life and Manners under the Early Empire*, trans. J. H. Freese and L. A. Magnus, 3 vols. (London: Routledge, 1908–13), 2: 41–62; Louis Robert, *Les Gladiateurs dans l'Orient grec* (Limoges, 1940; reprint, Amsterdam: Adolf Hakkert, 1971); J.P.V.D. Baldson, *Life and Leisure in Ancient Rome* (London: Bodley Head, 1969), 288–302; Alan Cameron, *Circus Factions: Blues and Greens at Rome and Byzantium* (Oxford: Clarendon Press, 1976), 59–60; Paul Veyne, *Le pain et le cirque: Sociologie historique d'un pluralisme politique* (Paris: Éditions du Seuil, 1976), 170n66, 290, 417–18.

23 Taylor, *Party Politics*, 30–31; Friedländer, *Roman Life*, 2: 41.

24 Inscriptions at Pompeii, a town south of Capua, in honor of gladiators are reproduced from the *Corpus Inscriptionum Latinarum* and translated by Shaw in his *Spartacus*.

25 Baldson, *Life and Leisure*, 300–1; Robert, *Gladiateurs*, 305–6.

26 Appian, *Roman Civil Wars*, 1, 14, in Wiedemann, *Slavery*, 220.

27 Plutarch, *Crassus*, in Wiedemann, *Slavery*, 216.

28 Davis, *Problem of Slavery*, chap. 3; Bradley, *Slavery and Society*, 134–35.

29 Plutarch, *Crassus*, in Wiedemann, *Slavery*, 216.

30 On these earlier revolts, see Wiedemann, *Slavery*, 198–215; Bradley, *Slavery and Rebellion*, chaps. 3–4; and Shaw, *Spartacus*.

31 Wiedemann, *Slavery*, 216.

32 Ibid., 217, 219; Salles, *Spartacus*, 20–30.

33 Taylor, *Party Politics*, 76–90.

34 On Kubrick's use of space in *Paths of Glory*, see the insightful pages of Thomas Allen Nelson, *Kubrick: Inside a Film Artist's Maze* (Bloomington: Indiana University Press, 1982), 37–53.

35 Gelis, *Film Director*, 296–97.

36 Bradley, *Slaves and Masters*, chap. 2; Keith R. Bradley, *Discovering the Roman Family: Studies in Roman Social History* (New York and Oxford: Oxford University Press, 1991), 62; Suzanne Dixon, *The Roman Family* (Baltimore: Johns Hopkins University Press, 1992), 10, 53–54, 113, 128–29.

37 Baxter, *Kubrick*, 164–66.

Chapter 3: Ceremony and Revolt: Burn! *and* The Last Supper

1 Interview of Gillo Pontecorvo with Julio Medem, <www.ofcs. org/article10.html>. On Gillo Pontecorvo, see Massimo Ghirelli, *Gillo Pontecorvo*, special issue of *Il Castoro Cinema* 60 (December 1978); Dan Georgakas and Lenny Rubenstein, eds., *The Cineaste Interviews on the Art and Politics of the Cinema* (Chicago: Lake View Press, 1983), 87–97 (interview of Gillo Pontecorvo with Harold Kalishman, 1974), 307–12 (interview of Gillo Pontecorvo with Corinne Luca); and John J. Michalczyk, *The Italian Political Film-makers* (Rutherford, NJ: Fairleigh Dickinson University Press; London and Toronto: Associated University Presses, 1986), chap. 5. A newly published work is Irene Bignardi, *Memorie estorte a uno smemorata: Vita di Gillo Pontecorvo* (Milan: Feltrinelli, 1999).

2 Medem interview. Exactly how much change was possible through film was open to doubt, however: "Honestly, I don't think a film can do very much. But . . . if the little we do is on a large front, I think it helps. If you reach a large front of people, you make a little step forward." Georgakas and Rubenstein, eds., *Interviews*, 96.

3 Michalczyk, *Filmmakers*, 184–86; Ghirelli, *Pontecorvo*, 19–21, 60; Medem interview.

4 Ghirelli, *Pontecorvo*, 18, 75; Georgakas and Rubenstein, eds., *Interviews*, 90–91; John D.H. Downing, ed., *Film and Politics in the Third World* (Brooklyn: Autonomedia, 1987), 271 (on the Englishman Richard Madden, commissioner of an Arbitration Tribunal in Cuba regarding the treatment of slaves, as a model for Sir William Walker's role in *Burn!*). Initially, Pontecorvo had intended a Spanish colony, but his distributors, United Artists, fearing a reaction from the Spanish market, had him change the colony to Portuguese!

5 First published in 1938, *The Black Jacobins* came out in French translation in 1949 (*Les Jacobins noirs* [Paris: Gallimard]) and in Italian translation in 1968 (*I Jacobini Neri* [Milan: Feltrinelli]).

6 C.L.R. James, *The Black Jacobins: Toussaint L'Ouverture and the San Domingo Revolution*, 2nd ed. (New York: Vintage Books, 1989), 18, 86; Joan Dayan, *Haiti, History, and the Gods* (Berkeley: Univer-

sity of California Press, 1995), 29–65; Eugene Genovese, *From Rebellion to Revolution: Afro-American Slave Revolts in the Making of the Modern World* (Baton Rouge: Louisiana State University Press, 1979), 28–32.

7 Marlon Brando with Robert Lindsey, *Brando: Songs My Mother Taught Me* (New York: Random House, 1994), 320 and chap. 46, for his description of the shooting and his quarrels with Pontecorvo. Pontecorvo has also commented on the fights he had with Brando during the filming, but both men continue to admire each other's work enormously. Ghirelli, *Pontecorvo*, 18; Medem interview; Brando, *Brando*, 320, 330.

8 Georgakas and Rubenstein, eds., *Interviews*, 89. Pontecorvo feared that his intentions in this scene were not clear to the public, "and it's a pity because it is only a question of three words or three phrases more to make it clear" (91).

9 Dayan, *Haiti*, 155.

10 Frantz Fanon's *Les Damnés de la terre* (Paris: François Maspero, 1961) helped form Pontecorvo's understanding of the rage and divisiveness among colonized peoples. Ghirelli, *Pontecorvo*, 75.

11 Michalczyk, *Filmmakers*, 187.

12 Julienne Burton, ed., *Cinema and Social Change in Latin America: Conversations with Filmmakers* (Austin: University of Texas Press, 1986), interview with Tomás Gutiérrez Alea, 124, 127. Other interviews with Gutiérrez Alea: Gerardo Chijona, "*La Última Cena*: Entrevista a Tomás Gutiérrez Alea," *Cine Cubano* 93 (1977): 81–89; and Maria do Rosário Caetano, *Cineastas Latin-Americanos. Entrevistas e Filmes* (São Paolo: Estação Liberdade, 1997), 151–58. An excerpt from his 1988 book, *The Viewer's Dialectic*, appears in Michael T. Martin, ed., *New Latin American Cinema*, 2 vols. (Detroit: Wayne State University Press, 1997), 108–31. See also John Downing, "Four Films of Tomás Gutiérrez Alea," in Downing, ed., *Film and Politics*, 279–301.

13 Julianne Burton and Gary Crowdus, "Sergio Giral," in Downing, ed., *Film and Politics*, 269–74. It would be interesting to know how this generation of Cuban historians viewed the earlier work on Cuban slavery by the historical anthropologist Fernando Ortiz Fernández, such as *Hampa afro-cubana. Los negros esclavos*

(Havana: Revista Bimestre Cubana, 1916), a remarkable and well-documented study of slaves and slavery. He did say that Cuban slavery was less cruel than that in British and French colonies, but did not ignore its negative features (179–80).

14 Manuel Moreno Fraginals, *The Sugarmill: The Socioeconomic Complex of Sugar in Cuba, 1760–1860*, trans. Cedric Belfrage (New York and London: Monthly Review Press, 1976), 9–12.

15 Moreno Fraginals, *Sugarmill*, 53–54 and Part 3. Moreno Fraginals now lives in Miami; his influence on both Latin American and American scholarship has been considerable. See also on the growth of slavery and the sugar plantation economy in Cuba, Franklin Knight, *Slave Society in Cuba during the Nineteenth Century* (Madison: University of Wisconsin Press, 1970), chap. 2; Manuel Moreno Fraginals, Frank Moya Pons, and Stanley Engerman, eds., *Between Slavery and Free Labor: The Spanish-Speaking Caribbean in the Nineteenth Century* (Baltimore: Johns Hopkins University Press, 1985), 280; and Laird W. Bergad, Fe Iglesias García, and María del Carmen Barcia, *The Cuban Slave Market, 1790–1880* (Cambridge: Cambridge University Press, 1995), chap. 2.

16 Phone conversation with Teresa Pedraza Moreno and Manuel Moreno Fraginals, 22 November 1999. Dr. Moreno Fraginals has kindly recalled for me the contents of the document in the Cuban archives reporting the revolt (Real Consulado, leg. 150, no. 7405), which is only briefly described in his *Sugarmill*.

17 This story is related to a tale type found in West Africa, the American South, and the Caribbean about family members selling each other (often the mother is to be sold) during a famine. William Bascom, *African Folktales in the New World* (Bloomington and Indianapolis: Indiana University Press, 1992), chap. 11.

18 On Olofin and creation tales, see Simeón Teodoro Diaz Favelo, *Cincuenta y un Pattakies afroamericanos* (Caracas: Monte Agila Editores, 1983), 10, 13–14, 16–31, 99.

19 Letter from Manuel Moreno Fraginals and Teresa Pedraza Moreno, 22 November 1999. A full summary of the code of 1789 is given by Herbert S. Klein, *Slavery in the Americas: A Comparative Study of Virginia and Cuba* (Chicago: University of Chicago Press, 1967), 78–85 and 84n65.

20 Moreno Fraginals, *Sugarmill*, 51–59; Chijona, "Entrevista," 83. Gutiérrez Alea spoke with pride of the historical research behind his film.

21 Moreno Fraginals, *Sugarmill*, 30–33, 54–55, 148, 152; letter from Moreno Fraginals and Pedraza Moreno, 22 November 1999; Knight, *Slave Society*, 76–77, 106–12; Nicolás Duque de Estrada, *Explicación de la doctrina cristiana acomodada a la capacidad de los negros bozales*, ed. Javier Laviña (Barcelona: Sendai, 1989), 74–75, 102–03, 109–11: some of the priest's teachings in the film are taken from Duque de Estrada's catechism, first published in Havana in 1797.

22 Letter from Moreno Fraginals and Pedraza Moreno, 22 November 1999; Chijona, "Entrevista," 82.

23 Letter from Moreno Fraginals and Pedraza Moreno, 22 November 1999.

24 Ortiz Fernández, *Negros esclavos*, 238–39; Knight, *Slave Society*, 63; Estaban Montejo, *Biografía de un Cimarrón*, ed. Miguel Barnet (Havana: Instituto de Etnología y Folklore, 1966), 17, 32–37; *The Autobiography of a Runaway Slave*, ed. Miguel Barnet, trans. Jocasta Innes (London: Bodley Head, 1968), 16–17, 33–38; Chijona, "Entrevista," 83–84. On creation tales and other tales about the high god Olofin, see note 18 above.

25 Montejo, *Biografía*, 42; *Autobiography*, 43–44.

26 Bascom, *African Folktales*, chap. 1: "Oba's Ear: A Yoruba Myth in Cuba and Brazil."

27 Phone conversation with Moreno Fraginals and Pedraza Moreno, 22 November 1999.

28 Among many studies of this process are Victor Turner, *The Ritual Process: Structure and Anti-Structure* (Chicago: University of Chicago Press, 1968); Natalie Zemon Davis (NZD), *Society and Culture in Early Modern France* (Stanford: Stanford University Press, 1975), chaps. 4–5; Barbara Babcock, ed., *The Reversible World: Symbolic Inversion in Art and Society* (Ithaca: Cornell University Press, 1978); Emmanuel Le Roy Ladurie, *Le Carnaval de Romans: de la Chandeleur au Mercredi des Cendres, 1579–1580* (Paris: Gallimard, 1979), *Carnival in Romans*, English translation by Mary Feeney (New York: Brazillier, 1979); Edward Muir, *Ritual in Early Modern Europe* (Cambridge: Cambridge University Press, 1997).

29 Letter of Moreno Fraginals and Pedraza Moreno, 23 November
    1999.

30 Ortiz Fernández, *Negros esclavos*, 396–423, especially 413, the wit-
    ness of Alexander Humboldt on the Cuban *cimarrones* in 1788–90;
    Javier Laviña, "Introducción" to Duque de Estrada, *Doctrina*, 30
    (distribution of slaves by sex and origin, 1746–90); Moreno Fragi-
    nals, *Sugarmill*, 142; Knight, *Slave Society*, 78–80. In *The Last Sup-
    per*, only one of the twelve slaves, Ambrosio, is the son of a slave
    woman, Encarnacion, who works on the count's plantation. She
    says that she doesn't know who his father is.

Chapter 4: *Witnesses of Trauma:* Amistad *and* Beloved

1 William Bascom, *African Folktales in the New World* (Bloomington
   and Indianapolis: Indiana University Press, 1992), chap. 11.

2 Interview with Toni Morrison by NZD, 7 October 1999.

3 Alhafi Sir Abubakar Tafawa Balewa, *Shaihu Umar*, trans. Mervin
   Hiskett (Princeton, NJ: Markus Wiener, 1989); Caryl Phillips,
   Cambridge (London: Bloomsbury, 1991), Part II, the memoir of
   Olumide from Guinea, especially 134–39; Derek Walcott, *Omeros*
   (New York: Farrar Straus Giroux, 1990), 130–49.

4 I have consulted Donald J. Waters, *Strange Ways and Sweet Dreams:
   Afro-American Folklore from the Hampton Institute* (Boston: G.K.
   Hall, 1983); Roger D. Abrahams, *Afro-American Folktales: Stories
   from Black Traditions in the New World* (New York: Pantheon
   Books, 1985); and Bascom, *African Folktales*.

5 Olaudah Equiano, *The Interesting Narrative of the Life of Olaudah
   Equiano Written by Himself*, ed. Robert J. Allison (Boston: Bedford
   Books, 1995), 55–56; Nancy Prince, *A Black Woman's Odyssey
   through Russia and Jamaica: The Narrative of Nancy Prince*, with an
   introduction by Ronald G. Walters (Princeton, NJ: Markus
   Wiener Publishers, 1995), 1–3; Jacob Stroyer, *My Life in the
   South* (1898), reprinted in William Loren Katz, ed., *Flight from the
   Devil: Six Slave Narratives* (Trenton, NJ: Africa World Press,
   1996), 159.

6 George Rawick, ed., *The American Slave: A Composite Autobiography*, 19 vols. (Westport, Conn.: Greenwood Publishing Company, 1972), vol. 2, part 2, 34; vol. 4, part 2, 163.

7 Edward M. Bruner, "Tourism in Ghana: The Representation of Slavery and the Return of the Black Diaspora," *American Anthropologist* 98 (1996): 290–304 (cites Richard Wright's description of his visit to Elmina in his *Black Power* of 1954). See also the response of Jean Augustine, a Canadian member of parliament, born in Grenada, to her recent visit to the slave market on Gorée Island in Sénégal: "I was moved. I was emotional. I was angry . . . It brought several things home to me in a very, very ugly way . . . These people had no choice . . . They had to be herded. How hot it must have been. And the children, all by themselves" (*Globe and Mail*, 9 November 1999, A4). In the interesting new collection edited by Maria Diedrich, Henry Louis Gates Jr., and Carl Pedersen, *Black Imagination and the Middle Passage* (New York: Oxford University Press, 1999), the focus is on hybridization of African and American culture—a cultural middle ground—rather than on the Middle Passage itself.

8 Steven Spielberg et al., *Amistad: "Give Us Free"* (New York: Newmarket Press, 1998), 9, 13. The best historical study of the *Amistad* affair is Howard Jones, *Mutiny on the "Amistad": The Saga of a Slave Revolt and Its Impact on American Abolition, Law, and Diplomacy* (New York: Oxford University Press, 1987).

9 Spielberg et al., *Amistad*, 16, 127.

10 The credits to *Amistad* thank several scholars who have made important contributions to the study of and resistance to slavery, including John Hope Franklin, Rebecca Scott, Howard Jones, Clifton Johnson, who originated the Amistad Research Center and who was an active consultant on the script, and Henry Louis Gates, who read the script at some point (*Amistad*, 42, 51, 123). Rebecca Scott was asked for advice about dress and the *mise-en-scène* for the scenes in Cuba (phone communication to NZD, 8 November 1999). In his two-day visit to Dream Works, Howard Jones watched the shooting, met Steven Spielberg and others, and was told by Debbie Allen how much his scholarly book was appreciated and used, but his advice was not sought about the film itself

(Howard Jones, "A Historian Goes to Hollywood: The Spielberg Touch," *Perspectives* 35 [(December 1997): 25–28]. Arthur Abraham, who was consulted throughout, had previously spent a year at the Amistad Research Center in New Orleans. He is author of *Mende Government and Politics under Colonial Rule* (Freetown: Sierra Leone University Press, 1978) and of a pamphlet entitled *The Amistad Revolt* (Freetown: USIS, 1987).

11 Spielberg et al., *Amistad*, 18, 38–39, 48–49, 54–56.

12 The role played by the British naval officer in the film was actually filled by the British abolitionist Richard Madden, who had served on a Spanish-British committee to put a stop to the slave trade and had acted for several years as the superintendent of liberated Africans in Havana (Jones, *Mutiny*, 99–100, 104–9). Madden was also one of the figures who inspired the role of Sir William Walker in *Burn!* (see note 4 to chapter 3).

13 Spielberg et al., *Amistad*, 12; Jones, *Mutiny*, 39–40; Bertram Wyatt-Brown, *Lewis Tappan and the Evangelical War against Slavery* (Cleveland: Case Western Reserve University Press, 1969), chap. 11, and 217, 292 (on James W.C. Pennington). Pennington was installed as pastor of the Fifth Congregational Church of Hartford in July 1840, where he preached sermons against the fugitive slave act, among many other subjects (*Covenants Involving Moral Wrong Are Not Obligatory upon Man: A Sermon Delivered in the Fifth Congregational Church Hartford, on Thanksgiving Day, November 17, 1842* [Hartford: J.C. Wells, 1842]). He was the author of *A Text Book of the Origin and History of the Colored People* (Hartford: L. Skinner, 1841) and a frequent contributor to the black abolitionist periodical *The Colored American*.

14 *The Colored American*, 28 September 1839. Jones, *Mutiny*, 35–37, 69–70, 76–79, 96–98. Nor was Judson, the actual judge at the second trial, a Catholic; he was the son of a Protestant minister (phone conversation with Howard Jones, 8 November 1999). Creating a young Catholic judge for the second trial—Judge Coglin—was an effort by the filmmakers to be inclusive and to suggest parallels between the way religion operated in the life of a vulnerable outsider and in the lives of the African outsiders looking at Bible pictures together. Other small changes were made in

the historical evidence: for instance, the judge at the second trial did not order the arrest of Ruiz and Montez for slave trading. They had already been arrested in October 1839 when Lewis Tappan arranged civil suits against them for Cinqué and a fellow African, Fuliwa, on charges of assault and false imprisonment. Montez was released and went back to Cuba, where Ruiz joined him after a four-month imprisonment (Jones, *Mutiny*, 85–94).

15 John Quincy Adams, *Memoirs of John Quincy Adams, Comprising Portions of His Diary from 1795 to 1848*, ed. Charles Francis Adams, 12 vols. (Philadelphia: J.B. Lippincott, 1874–77), 10: 133–35: "That which now absorbs a great part of my time and all my good feelings is the case of fifty-three [sic] African negroes taken at sea, off Montauk Point . . . and brought into the port of New London. These negros were a fresh importation of slaves from Africa into the Havanna against the laws of Spain and her treaties with Great Britain" (1 October 1839). Jones, *Mutiny*, 81–82.

16 Adams, *Memoirs*, 10: 358–60; Simon Schama, "Clio at the Multiplex," *The New Yorker*, 19 January 1998, 38.

17 *The Colored American*, 5 October 1839.

18 Spielberg et al., *Amistad*, 50.

19 Jones, *Mutiny*, 43.

20 Ibid., 123.

21 Abraham, *Mende Government*, 18–30, 161–62; Kenneth Little, *The Mende of Sierra Leone: A West African People In Transition* (London: Routledge and Keegan Paul, 1967), 37–39; Suzanne Miers and Igor Kopytoff, eds., *Slavery in Africa: Historical and Anthropological Perspectives* (Madison: University of Wisconsin Press, 1977): on Sierra Leone, see especially John J. Grace, "Slavery and Emancipation among the Mende in Sierra Leone," 415–31, and Carol P. MacCormack, "Wono: Institutionalized Dependency in Sherbro Descent Groups (Sierra Leone)," 181–203; E.S.D. Fomin and Victor Julius Ngoh, *Slave Settlements in the Banyang Country, 1800–1950* (Lembe, Cameroon: University of Buea Publications, 1998); Abubakar Tafawa Balewa, *Shaihu Umar*.

22 Covey himself knew this difference by experience: seized from his parents' house as a boy, he had been sold to a Mende chief, for whose wife he had planted rice, a woman who had treated him

"with great kindness." After three years he was sold to a Portuguese and endured four days on a slaver, until his ship was captured by a British patrol vessel and the Africans were released (silhouettes and summary of the testimony of the *Amistad* Africans by John W. Barber, *A History of the Amistad Captives* [1840], reprinted in facsimile in Mary Cable, *Black Odyssey: The Case of the Slave Ship "Amistad"* [New York: Viking Press, 1971], appendix I).

23 Ibid.

24 Jones, *Mutiny*, 24; Equiano, *Life*, 56–57.

25 Spielberg et al., *Amistad*, 18, 40.

26 Anthony J. Gittins, *Mende Religion* (Studi Instituti Anthropos, 41) (Nettetal: Steyler Verlag, 1988), 57. Another custom is suggested during Baldwin's first visit to the prison. The guards want to place a table for the lawyer so he can take notes. The Africans squabble among themselves according to regional difference within Mendedom about not wanting the table to be located in their part of the yard: the Mende as against the Temne men as against the Sherbro men. The Africanist Martin Klein doubts that in the circumstances of the New Haven prison these territorial boundaries would have been maintained: Africans established new groupings in the circumstances in which they found themselves in America, some of them even being formed on slave ships.

27 Adams, *Memoirs*, 19: 360 (on three Africans reading a chapter of the New Testament aloud, though "very indifferently"); Jones, *Mutiny*, 157–58, 248n8; *The Colored American*, 27 February 1841.

28 Barber, *Amistad Captives*, in Cable, *Black Odyssey*, appendix I (entry on Shuma); Jones, *Mutiny*, 42, 149; Wyatt-Brown, *Tappan*, 207; Gittins, *Mende Religion*, 45–52. The Union Missionary Society—later renamed the American Missionary Association—grew out of the collaboration of the black minister James Pennington and the *Amistad* committee. Pennington founded the society in the late summer of 1841, at the same time he was helping Tappan raise money for the return of the Africans to their homes. Once the *Amistad* committee merged with the Missionary Society, Tappan and Simon Jocelyn took control from the black founders, leaving them in only "minor and honorary posts" (Wyatt-Brown, *Tappan*, 292, especially citing the 1958 doctoral dissertation of

Clifton Herman Johnson, who later became a consultant for the film *Amistad*). The book that Debbie Allen optioned in 1984 when she hoped to make the film was William Owens's somewhat novelistic account *Black Mutiny* (Spielberg et al., *Amistad*, 14; William Owens, *Black Mutiny: The Revolt on the Schooner Amistad* [Philadelphia and Boston: Pilgrim Press, 1968]). It has a preface by the general secretary of the American Missionary Association. Even telling the story partially from the vantage point of the Missionary Society could lead to interesting conflict and complexity.

29 Little, *Mende*, 28–32, 118–26, 175–98, 240–53; Abraham, *Mende Government*, 30–38; Gittins, *Mende Religion*, 147–52; Jones, *Mutiny*, 44.

30 Barber, *Amistad Captives*, in Cable, *Black Odyssey*, appendix I. The hunter Pie was a Temne, one of the non-Mende people living in Mendeland. On *Schindler's List* and the character of Schindler, see the valuable chapter of Joseph McBride, *Steven Spielberg: A Biography* (New York: Simon and Schuster, 1997), chap. 16 and p. 436.

31 Gittins, *Mende Religion*, chap. 4 and p. 67.

32 Sean Wilentz, "The Mandarin and the Rebel," *The New Republic*, 22 December 1997, 25–34, a splendid essay on the entire career and person of John Quincy Adams, including an evaluation of the film *Amistad*. Adams, *Memoirs*, 10: 63 (13 December 1838).

33 Adams, *Memoirs*, 10: 373 (12 December 1840); 383 (27 December 1840); 440 (5 March 1841); 454 (29 April 1841).

34 Argument of John Quincy Adams before the Supreme Court of the United States in the case of the United States, Appellants, vs. Cinque, and others Africans . . . Delivered on the 24th of February and 1st of March 1841. Professor Howard Jones has kindly provided me with a copy of this argument, initially published in 1841. For a discussion of and quotation from the argument, see Jones, *Mutiny*, 172–81; and Adams's comments on the testimony in *Memoirs*, 10: 430–31 (23–24 February 1841); 435 (1 March 1841).

35 Adams chose a rather odd case of resistance to tyranny with which to compare the revolt of the Africans. Drawn initially from Thucydides, *Peloponnesian War*, 5: 54–58, the story tells of two Athenian lovers, Aristogiton and Harmodius, who were offended when Hipparchus, brother and associate of the reigning tyrant Hippias,

tried to woo Harmodius away from Aristogiton. The two men organized a small conspiracy to slay the tyrant, failed, and were slain themselves. Subsequently the fearful Hippias cracked down on the citizens of Athens and put many to death, whereupon the Athenians began to regard Harmodius and Aristogiton with some appreciation. Hippias was deposed a few years later under the leadership of another ruling family, which had been banished.

36 *The Colored American*, 6 March 1841, report from Charles B. Ray, Washington, 1 March 1841.

37 See, for instance, Johannes Fabian, *Time and the Other: How Anthropology Makes Its Other* (New York: Columbia University Press, 1983), and Walter D. Mignolo, *The Darker Side of the Renaissance: Literacy, Territoriality, and Colonization* (Ann Arbor: University of Michigan Press, 1995).

38 NZD interview with Toni Morrison, 7 October 1999; Middleton Harris et al., *The Black Book* (New York: Random House, 1974), 10.

39 Mervyn Rothstein, "Toni Morrison, in Her New Novel, Defends Women," *New York Times*, 26 August 1987, C17; NZD interview with Toni Morrison, 7 October 1999. See the discussion of these issues also in Elizabeth Fox-Genovese, *Unspeakable Things Unspoken: Ghosts and Memories in the Narratives of African-American Women* (The 1992 Elsa Goveia Memorial Lecture) (Mona, Jamaica: University of West Indies, Department of History, 1992).

40 Herbert Guttman, *The Black Slave Family in Slavery and Freedom, 1750–1925* (New York: Pantheon Books, 1976), is the master study: see chaps. 3–4, on naming practices; 274–76, on wedding customs. Charles Joyner, *Down by the Riverside: A South Carolina Slave Community* (Urbana and Chicago: University of Illinois Press, 1984), 138–39; Elizabeth Fox-Genovese, *Within the Plantation Household: Black and White Women of the Old South* (Chapel Hill and London: University of North Carolina Press, 1988). Fox-Genovese stresses the pressure of the plantation household and the powers of owners on the black family, but comments also: "Evidence reveals that a concern for family held consuming importance for Afro-Americans both in slavery times and after emancipation" (31–32, 93–95, 177–78, 190, 297–98). Deborah Gray White, *Ar'n't I a Woman? Female Slaves in the Plantation South*

(New York: W.W. Norton, 1985), 68–70; Deborah Gray White, "Female Slaves in the Plantation South," in Edward D.C. Campbell Jr. and Kym S. Rice, eds., *Before Freedom Came: African-American Life in the Antebellum South* (Charlottesville: University Press of Virginia; Richmond: Museum of the Confederacy, 1991), 101–21; Rawick, ed., *American Slave*, vol. 16, part 2, 33, 39 (a Kentucky master says after selling a slave's wife, "Don't worry, you can get another one"), 64, 75, 104; part 4, 28; George Rawick, ed., *American Slave: A Composite Autobiography. Supplement*, 12 vols. (Westport, Conn.: Greenwood Publishing Company, 1977), Series 1, vol. 5, 395, 408–10 (example of a Kentucky master "a litle mo' human den some of de slave owners": he bought whole families and did not allow them to be separated), 430.

41 John Hope Franklin and Loren Schweninger, *Runaway Slaves: Rebels on the Plantation* (New York: Oxford University Press, 1999), xiv, 49–67, 210–13, 262; Fox-Genovese, *Plantation Household*, 319–23, 387–89; White, "Female Slaves," 107; Rawick, ed., *American Slave*, vol. 16, part 2, 31, 71.

42 Steven Weisenburger's splendid book on the subject appeared in 1998: *Modern Medea: A Family Story of Slavery and Child-Murder from the Old South* (New York: Hill and Wang, 1998); Rothstein, "Morrison."

43 Toni Morrison, *Beloved* (New York: Alfred A. Knopf, 1987), 73.

44 Ibid., 75, 210–11; see also Claudine Raynaud, "The Poetics of Abjection in *Beloved*," in Diedrich, Gates, and Pedersen, *Black Imagination*, chap. 6.

45 Spielberg et al., *Amistad*, 9; George Mair, *Oprah Winfrey: The Real Story* (New York: Birch Lane Press, 1994), chaps. 1–3, 18, and 84–85; Janet Lowe, *Oprah Winfrey Speaks* (New York: John Wiley, 1998), 19–30, 130–33; McBride, *Spielberg*, 371–71 (on Winfrey in *The Color Purple*).

46 "Oprah's Power to Be Beloved," *The Sunday Sun*, 4 October 1998, 8–9; Richard Corliss, "Bewitching Beloved," and Ron Stodghill, "Daring to Go There," in *Time* (Canadian edition), 5 October 1998, 51, 57; bell hooks, "The Oppositional Gaze: Black Female Spectators," in Sue Thornham, ed., *Feminist Film Theory: A Reader* (New York: New York University Press, 1999), 319.

47　NZD interview with Toni Morrison, 7 October 1999.

48　Michael Bliss and Christina Banks, *What Goes Around Comes Around: The Films of Jonathan Demme* (Carbondale and Edwardsville: Southern Illinois University Press, 1996), 80–82, 84, 94, 108, 124, 136. This otherwise excellent book is too critical of shortcomings in the moral vision of *Silence of the Lambs*. Interviewed in 1990, Demme said he hoped to make films on "black subjects, racial subjects, interracial subjects. We want to make movies that have strong appeal to audiences other than just white people" (146).

49　NZD interview with Toni Morrison, 7 October 1999.

50　White, "Female Slaves," 105–6; White, *Ar'n't I a Woman?* 99–114; Fox-Genovese, *Plantation Household*, 148–49.

51　"All the Pretty Little Horses," in Harris et al., *Black Book*, 65.

52　Fox-Genovese, *Plantation Household*, 323–24, 456n58; White, *Ar'n't I a Woman?* 87–89; White, "Female Slaves," 113; Rawick, ed., *American Slave: A Composite Autobiography. Supplement*, series 1, vol. 9, part 4, 1449; vol. 11, part 1, 54; Harriet A. Jacobs, *Incidents in the Life of a Slave Girl, Written by Herself*, ed. Jean Fagan Yellin (Cambridge, Mass.: Harvard University Press, 1987), 62.

53　Weisenburger, *Modern Medea*, 86, 171–72, 253–57 (the literary background in antislavery writing to attitudes like that of Lucy Stone). Garner's lawyer, the abolitionist John Joliffe, blamed the Fugitive Slave Law, which "had driven a frantic mother to murder her own child, rather than see it carried back to the seething Hell of American slavery" (124). *Provincial Freeman*, 2 February 1856.

54　Bliss and Banks, *Films of Jonathan Demme*, 3.

55　Waters, *Strange Ways*, 297–98, 300–1, 345–46; Rawick, ed., *American Slave*, vol. 16, part 2, 36, 58, 61, 64, 67, 109.

56　Rawick, ed., *American Slave*, vol. 16, part 2, 94, 109; Waters, *Strange Ways*, 202, 278. Demme had experimented with the use of red light in *Philadelphia* to express the desperate and ecstatic state of mind of the dying Andy as he listens to a favorite operatic aria. The technique is carried much further in *Beloved*.

57　Morrison, *Beloved*, 62. Baby Suggs, too, has unwanted children by white men, but Sethe has the "amazing luck of six whole years of marriage to [Halle] who had fathered every one of her children" (23). Gerda Lerner, ed., *Black Women in America: A Documentary*

History (New York: Pantheon Books, 1972), 61 (quoting Levi Coffin's reminiscence on the Margaret Garner case); Weisenburger, *Modern Medea*, 44, 47–49, 157, 242–43.

58 Linda Krumholz, "The Ghosts of Slavery: Historical Recovery in Toni Morrison's *Beloved*," *African American Review* 26 (1992): 400–3.

59 Eugene Genovese, *Roll, Jordan, Roll: The World the Slaves Made* (New York: Vintage Books, 1974), 209–80; Joyner, *Down by the Riverside*, chap. 5; Charles Joyner, "The World of Plantation Slaves," in Campbell and Rice, eds., *Before Freedom*, 73–77; Albert J. Raboteau, *Slave Religion: The "Invisible Institution" in the Antebellum South* (New York: Oxford University Press, 1978), 212–19, 231–39 (prophetesses on 238); Fox-Genovese, *Plantation World*, 331, 457n74; Rawick, ed., *African Slave*, vol. 4, part 1, 4–8; part 2, 294; vol. 16, part 2, 36–38, 46 (John Anderson: "When I was growing up my mammy always believed in making her own medicine, and doctored the whole family with the roots she dug herself"), 90ff, 98–99; part 4, 42–43. Jacobs, *Incidents in the Life of a Slave Girl*, 67 and chap. 13; Linda Bryant does not preach, but does teach another slave to read the Bible (72–73). Nell Irwin Painter, *Sojourner Truth: A Life, a Symbol* (New York: W.W. Norton, 1996), 32, 42–44.

60 Joyner, *Down by the Riverside*, 160. There is heart imagery also in Raboteau, *Slave Religion*, 217: "then everyone's heart was in tune, and when they called on God they made heaven ring."

61 NZD interview with Toni Morrison, 7 October 1999. Oprah Winfrey's journal kept during the filming, *Time* (Canadian edition), 5 October 1998, 54.

62 Weisenburger, *Modern Medea*, 75.

63 Ibid., 278; "The Slave Margaret," *Provincial Freeman*, 5 April 1856.

Chapter 5: Telling the Truth

1 On genre categories and their revision in film, see Louis Giannetti, *Understanding Movies*, 6th ed. (Englewood Cliffs, NJ: Prentice

Hall, 1993), 333–34. For a thoughtful definition of "epic" in film, see Derek Elley, *The Epic Film: Myth and History* (London: Routledge and Kegan Paul, 1984), 1–16.

2 A similar point could be made about the use of court ceremonial in films about kings and queens, as I hope to develop in a future study. Filmmakers loved to recreate such events even in the silent cinema, but it took historians a while to follow up the insights on the semiotic and political importance of royal ritual offered in the books by Marc Bloch, Ernst Kantorowicz, and Ralph Giesey. Marc Bloch, *Les Rois thaumaturges: Étude sur le caractère surnaturel attribué à la puissance royale particulièrement en France et en Angleterre* (Strasbourg and Paris: Librairie Istra, 1924); Ernst H. Kantorowicz, *The King's Two Bodies: A Study in Mediaeval Political Theology* (Princeton, NJ: Princeton University Press, 1957); Ralph Giesey, *The Royal Funeral Ceremony in Renaissance France* (Geneva: Librairie Droz, 1960).

3 Peter Biskind, ed., "On Movies, Money and Politics," *The Nation*, 5–12 April 1999, 20.

4 Steven Spielberg et al., *Amistad: "Give Us Free"* (New York: Newmarket Press, 1998), 10, 17, 127.

5 Ibid., 57–61, 64. Ruth Carter's costumes for the Africans are at their most successful when they are simplest and give that right "overall impression." Cinqué's ornate embroidered garb, worn at the session of the Supreme Court, is not what would have been provided him by the Christian abolitionists. But the whole episode never happened. Even after they were freed from Westville prison, the abolitionists were still insisting that the Africans wear humble dress: "'Hard Times' work clothes . . . in order to comply with the white man's notion of their station in life." By then, a Yale divinity instructor complained, the Mende wanted to dress like gentlemen. Bertram Wyatt-Brown, *Lewis Tappan and the Evangelical War against Slavery* (Cleveland: Press of Case Western Reserve University, 1969), 216–17.

6 The point I am making here about certain scenes in *Amistad* has been described by George M. Wilson as a general complaint against serious Hollywood films: "that they announce an investigation and present a wish-fulfilling spectacle instead." See his *Nar-*

ration in Light: Studies in Cinematic Point of View (Baltimore: Johns Hopkins University Press, 1986), 44.

7 John Quincy Adams, *Memoirs of John Quincy Adams, Comprising Portions of His Diary from 1795 to 1848*, ed. Charles Francis Adams, 12 vols. (Philadelphia: J.B. Lippincott, 1874–77), 10: 358, 373. Argument of John Quincy Adams before the Supreme Court of the United States in the case of the United States, Appellants, vs. Cinque, and others Africans . . . Delivered on the 24th of February and the 1st of March 1841, 43.

8 Paul Gilroy, *The Black Atlantic: Modernity and Double Consciousness* (Cambridge, Mass.: Harvard University Press, 1993), 21–25.

9 Initially published in the *Emancipator*, 25 March 1841 (but not, alas, noted by John Quincy Adams in his diary), this letter is quoted both by Arthur Abraham, *The Amistad Revolt* (Freetown: United States Information Service, 1987), 25–26, and by Howard Jones, *Mutiny on the "Amistad"* (New York and Oxford: Oxford University Press, 1987), 203. Abraham attributes it to Kali, one of the four children among the captives; Jones attributes it to Kale, a young man.

10 Cited from the *Liberator*, 3 December 1841, by Wyatt-Brown, *Lewis Tappan*, 219–20.

11 On the relation of evidence to storytelling in historical films, see the interesting dialogue between historian Eric Foner and director John Sayles in Mark C. Carnes et al., eds., *Past Imperfect: History According to the Movies* (New York: Henry Holt, 1995), 11–28.

12 George Perry, *Steven Spielberg* (London: Orion, 1998), 100.

13 I have tried to give attention to this question in my article, "'Any Attention to Persons Living or Dead': Film and the Challenge of Authenticity" (The Fifth Patricia Wise Lecture, American Film Institute), *Historical Journal of Film, Radio and Television* 8 (1988): 269–83. *Spartacus* has a disclaimer at the end of the final credits: "Similarity to actual persons living or dead is purely coincidental."

14 Thomas Wiedemann, *Greek and Roman Slavery* (London: Croom Helm, 1981), 215–20. Brent D. Shaw discusses Garibaldi's interest in Spartacus in the introduction to *Spartacus and the Roman Slave Wars: A Brief History with Documents* (Boston: Bedford Books, forthcoming). George Rawick, ed., *The American Slave: A Composite*

Autobiography, 19 vols. (Westport, Conn.: Greenwood Publishing Company, 1972), vol. 2, part 2, 149–51. Cinqué became known as "the Black Prince" before his return to Africa. Jones, *Mutiny*, 201.

15 Wilson, *Narration in Light*, chaps. 3, 5; David Bordwell, *Narration in the Fiction Film* (Madison: University of Wisconsin Press, 1985), 130–46 and chaps. 9–10; Robert Stam, *Reflexivity in Film and Literature* (New York: Columbia University Press, 1992), especially introduction and chap. 3.

16 Wyatt-Brown, *Lewis Tappan*, 220; William A. Owens, *Black Mutiny: The Revolt on the Schooner Amistad* (Philadelphia and Boston: Pilgrim Press, 1968), vii–xi.

17 Biskind, ed., "On Movies," 18.

Illustration Credits

Chapter 1

Photograph from *The Last Supper* © 1976 ICAIC. © 1977 ICAIC. Courtesy of ICAIC. Available in 16 mm and VHS from New Yorker Films.

Chapter 2

Photographs from *Spartacus* copyright © 2000 by Universal City Studios, Inc. Courtesy of Universal Studios Publishing Rights. All Rights Reserved.

Chapter 3

Photographs from *Burn!* © 1969 Pea Produzioni Europee Associate SAS. All Rights Reserved. Courtesy MGM Clip + Still.

Photographs from *The Last Supper* © 1976 ICAIC. © 1977 ICAIC. Courtesy of ICAIC. Available in 16 mm and VHS from New Yorker Films.

Chapter 4

Photographs by Andrew Cooper for the motion picture *Amistad* TM and © 1997 DreamWorks L.L.C., reprinted with permission by DreamWorks L.L.C.

Photographs for *Beloved* © Touchstone Pictures Company. All Rights Reserved. Photos: Ken Regan.

For assistance in obtaining the illustrations for this book I would like to thank the following people: Margaret Adamic, Debbie Allen, Neda Armian, Holly Clark, John Hope Franklin, Lisa Halliday, Piers Handling, Melissa Hendricks, Stacie Iverson and José Lopez.

Acknowledgments

I MET Barbara Frum in the mid-1960s, when both of us were exploring the role of women's education in Toronto. Her warmth, lively intellect, and commitment have stayed fresh in my mind as I wrote these pages for a series in her memory. I appreciate the invitation of the Barbara Frum Lectureship and the Department of History of the University of Toronto to deliver the lectures for the year 2000 in her honor, and especially want to thank Murray Frum for urging me to reflect here on historical film. Murray Frum and Nancy Lockhart have contributed much to a better understanding of film in Canada, and I am grateful for their encouragement on this project.

Among the greatest pleasures of *Slaves on Screen* was the opportunity to interview Toni Morrison, my Princeton colleague, about her book *Beloved* and the film based on it. Another delight was my interview and exchange of letters with Manuel Moreno Fraginals and Teresa Pedraza Moreno about Professor Moreno Fraginals's book *The Sugarmill* and his role as historical consultant for *The Last Supper*. Piers Handling and Wayne Clarkson of the Toronto International Film Festival generously listened to my ideas about history and film early in their formulation. I have also learned much about filmmaking in conversation with Aaron Davis. Many friends responded with alacrity to my scholarly queries and I thank them here: Roger Abrahams, Jeremy Adelman,

William Callahan, Simone Davis, Joan Dayan, Elizabeth Fox-Genovese, Marianne Hirsch, Michael Jiménez, Howard Jones, Martin Klein, Solimar Otero, David Prochaska, Aaron Retica, Teofilo Ruiz, Rebecca Scott, Robert Sklar, and Sean Wilentz. Kate McNairn and the personnel of the Audiovisual Library at the University of Toronto were helpful at every stage of my research, and it was also rewarding to work with the resources of the Toronto International Film Festival Library. John Barthel of Vintage Video gave me good advice, and the staff at Super Video 99 exhibited much patience in the extended use of cassettes.

My agent, Anne Engel, and Sarah Davies of Random House Canada gave warm support to the realization of *Slaves on Screen*. Rosemary Shipton's experienced eye and wonderful sense of language have added much to the quality of my text. It was also a pleasure to consult with Jennifer Armour on the cover design and see her artist's vision at work. I also extend my thanks to Gordon Robertson for the book's handsome interior design.

This book is dedicated to the memory of two fathers whose lives had links to the themes of *Slaves on Screen*. My father, Julian Leon Zemon, loved the theater and wrote plays and musicals in his spare time. He was at his happiest about my research when I served as historical consultant for the film *Le retour de Martin Guerre*. My husband's father, Horace Bancroft Davis, was descended from staunch abolitionists. His grandfather, Norwood Penrose Hallowell, was colonel to the Massachusetts 55th Regiment, black troops who fought against slavery in the Civil War. Horace Davis's own quest for justice was built on such forebears.

I first saw some of the films examined in *Slaves on Screen* while holding hands with Chandler Davis at the movies. It has been great fun to discuss with him the themes of history and film, savoring together these visions of and voices from the past.

CPSIA information can be obtained
at www.ICGtesting.com
Printed in the USA
LVHW080531160722
723467LV00006B/48